Devoto

76 Activities

That Touch the
Inner Spirit of Youth

Ric Stuecker with Suze Rutherford

Research Press
2612 North Mattis Avenue   Champaign, Illinois 61822
www.researchpress.com

Editing and Project Management: Lorna Cunkle, Sebastopol, California
Cover Design by Linda Brown, Positive I.D. Graphic Design, Inc.
Interior Design by WordWrap, Sebastopol, California
Printer: Von Hoffman Graphics, Inc.

ISBN 0-87822-474-2
Library of Congress Control Number 2001090290

To Barbara,
who inspires me and daily touches my inner spirit

And to Wayne,
who empowers me to do my work

Contents

Foreword ix

Preface xi

Acknowledgments xv

Part One   **Optimum Learning Environments** 1

Chapter 1   Hope 3

Chapter 2   Humor 13

Chapter 3   Heroes 17

Chapter 4   Head 25

Chapter 5   Heart 33

Part Two   **The Personal Journey** 37

Chapter 6   Basic Tools and Practices 39

Chapter 7   The Inner Me 47

Chapter 8   Heroes, Role Models, and Mentors 75

Chapter 9   Connecting with Others 91

Chapter 10   Mission Statement Workshop 123

Part Three   **Transformations** 135

Chapter 11   Girl into Woman, Boy into Man 137

Chapter 12   Stewardship 157

Chapter 13   Rites of Passage and Initiation 167

Appendix One   Character Education in Schools: The Resiliency, Youth
                      Development, Asset-Building Continuum 177

Appendix Two   Using *Reviving the Wonder* in the School Curriculum 185

Notes 209

Resources 213

Index of Activities 217

About the Authors 219

About National Training Associates 221

Foreword

Once upon a time, when culture was whole, it would initiate its youth into maturity using time-honored and carefully worked out methods designed to pass on deep spiritual truths and essential learning necessary for taking one's place as an adult in the community. Today, at a time when culture is fragmented almost beyond recognition (as part of this culture, we see only dimly the extent of this damage), youth are left more or less to their own devices to puzzle out the intricacies of this labyrinthine mess and to figure out how to find a place for themselves in its disintegrating fragments. The results of this are only too obvious: depression, suicide, eating disorders, substance abuse, fatal "accidents," school violence, sexual assaults, apathy, despair, numbness, and rampant cynicism among our adolescents.

Not having the benefit of the time-honored tools of integration— the "rites of passage" that mankind had at its disposal for thousands of years—the adults in our society have lately too often responded to these symptoms of cultural breakdown with broken-down methods of their own, including "zero tolerance" policies, as if saying "there will be no xyz" is sufficient to make it go away; psychoactive medications, which may be a sort of biochemical compensation for living in a non-whole world; incarceration, where juveniles are increasingly being treated like adults in courts of law; and "higher standards," as if raising the bar will somehow make everyone a little bit taller.

Reviving the Wonder: 76 Activities That Touch the Inner Spirit of Youth is a book that stands for something deeply redemptive in the midst of all these mischarted policies. I say it is redemptive because it is based upon the belief that only healthy adults working in a safe and healing space with youth can help them cross the bridge from childhood to maturity. This book is filled with activities, ideas, tips, and inspiration, designed to provide such a space within which healthy adults can help adolescents pick up the pieces that society left on the floor when it "dropped the bag" and failed its youngsters long ago. What is particularly refreshing about this book is that it acknowledges the wonder of adolescence. We're apt to forget this fact when we hear a litany of teenage troubles broadcast in the media. But the teenage years are times of great existential musings, aesthetic imaginings, intellectual explorations, and spiritual yearnings.

I have just been reading G. Stanley Hall's *Adolescence*, the book that pretty much "invented" the subject as a field of research in 1904 and I was enthralled by a recount of the adolescence of many great historical figures. The energy and passion of this time of life shows through in many of these biographies. Joan of Arc had her first visions at thirteen; Ben Franklin read poetry all night at the same age; Oliver Wendell Holmes had a passion for flowers, broke into poetry at fifteen, and "had very romantic attachments to certain trees in particular." Percy Shelly wandered by moonlight communing with the moon and stars. George Sand created plays and daydreams that were so intense that she often came back from the world of imagining to reality with a shock.

Hall wrote that "the best observers see but very little of what goes on in the youthful soul, the development of which is very largely subterranean. Only when the feelings erupt in some surprising way is the process manifest." This suggests that the art of relating to adolescence is a very delicate one—and the many helpful hints and guidelines in this book for sensitively working with youth should be a definite help here. We are apt to forget our own adolescence as we age. We need to remember our own times of poetry writing, nature worshipping, life-or-death romances, moody diatribes on politics, spiritual conversions, philosophical introspection, or other passionate endeavors during that critical time in our lives. Once we have made the bridge within ourselves between our own recovered adolescence and our lives as mature adults today, then we can make use of our own inner integration to more deeply connect with adolescents using the many marvelous activities contained in this positive and transformative book. My greatest respect goes out to those of you who are about to embark upon this sacred task of reviving the wonder in youth. As you engage in this process, you are doing nothing less than helping to heal profound dislocations in the structure of society itself.

THOMAS ARMSTRONG, PH.D.
AUTHOR OF *7 KINDS OF SMART: IDENTIFYING AND
DEVELOPING YOUR MULTIPLE INTELLIGENCES*

Preface

The wonder. What happens to the wonder in youth? The wonder that at one time led them to explore their world in all directions? To question explanations? To find out for themselves? To believe in their own authenticity and power? What happens to the joy found in any kindergarten classroom? The willingness to believe, to play with ideas, to ponder and think, to create without boundaries, to aspire to be and do wonderful things?

Unable to answer these questions and inspired by Mary Pipher's *Reviving Ophelia* and Michael Gurian's *The Wonder of Boys,* Suze Rutherford and I began to develop a retreat experience designed to help adolescents identify their life purpose and develop a plan for fulfilling that purpose. The premise behind the retreat and all the activities in this book is that boys and girls need connections with healthy men and women who can help them by discussing and modeling the principles and mores that will turn them into strong, responsible, and loving adults.

All children dream, hope, plan, aspire, and plot — even in the worst of situations. Read *The Diary of Anne Frank;* the joy and heartbreak she describes are filled with personal hopes, dreams, and aspirations. In twenty-first century U.S.A., school systems and communities often place youth who "don't fit in" into continuation schools, court schools, detention centers, and group homes. The stories of these young people are often heartbreaking. Many have been abused by the adults in their lives. They have been abandoned, labeled, and isolated from other, more "normal" youth. Looking at their lives in the most rational way, I find it difficult to understand why they do not lose all hope and become totally cynical. Yet, when given the opportunity, over and over they express personal aspirations, hopes, and dreams that are full of the language of accomplishment, positive outlook, and responsible living.

As mentors, advocates, teachers, promoters, trainers, ministers, and counselors, our job is to empower youth to foster dreams and aspirations, and to construct opportunities for them to pursue their vision of a hopeful future even when the likelihood of fulfillment seems dim and frail. I believe there is an inner spirit in youth — the same head-and-heart connection evident in all human beings. When connections are made at deep levels, all of a sudden a community is built that becomes something greater than the individuals within it. When these connections are made — within ourselves and with each other — dreams become reality.

This book of activities, techniques, and approaches is a guide for those who support youth in their journey out of childhood into the community of adults. Youth need initiation into a caring, adult culture where they can find acceptance and importance, and where they can develop a clear picture of what makes up a healthy and congruent man and woman. Michael Gurian and Mary Pipher eloquently argue that life's journey is a constantly renewing process. When we identify and examine the forces, directions, and principles at work at each stage of our journey, we then engage positively in the world around us based on those principles.

For a long time, according to both Gurian and Pipher, we've experienced a decrease in the number of positive role models available to our young people, along with an increase in both negative and sexist cultural images. As a result, girls and boys have a difficult time defining themselves as adults and productive members of society. Both are susceptible to creating false selves based on confusing definitions of femininity and masculinity. By the time they turn thirteen, most girls discover that their school life is increasingly girl-poisoning, and lose their natural confidence, spontaneity, and authenticity. During the same years, this false self can lead boys into inappropriate aggression, irresponsible sexuality, gang membership, and crime.

The uncomprehending adult community sees these maturational difficulties in terms of high rates of drug and alcohol use, sexually transmitted diseases, pregnancies, suicides, and antisocial manifestations like sexual harassment, bullying, and other random acts of violence. Those of us who work with youth on a daily basis have come to realize that boys and girls are different, and they have very different developmental needs. As much as each gender needs positive experiences with the opposite sex, they also need separate positive experiences. Girls need to recapture their wonder, joy, confidence, and energy as they evolve into authentic adult women. Boys need to find ways to satisfy their need for bonding as well as socially acceptable outlets for their competitiveness and aggressive tendencies.

Over the period of three years, Suze and I developed the activities in this book, tested them, and further developed our ideas as we worked with art therapists, storytellers, and others interested in enhancing the spirituality of youth. In September 1997, I was initiated into the Louisville New Warriors Community (a part of The ManKind Project), and I became a member of a group of adults who were meeting to implement the practices described by Stephen Covey in his books. I became aware of the resiliency research, especially as applied by Michelle Karns in her work on developing resilient youth, and then I learned about the Search Institute and its list of internal and external assets that lead to healthy development. As my own daughters reached adulthood, I learned from them, too, about the youthful longing for authenticity, meaningful work, and the power of self-reflection through a homemade sketchbook.

All these experiences helped frame my thinking as the Reviving the Wonder retreat became a valuable resource, not only for Suze and me but for many others who were putting together their own programs. As an expansion of our retreat planning, this book is designed so the various activities can be used to create your own event, retreat, or classroom lessons. There is enough material here for an entire course on exploring the inner spirit, defining gender, creating community, expanding leadership, and doing service. I have taught such classes in six- to eight-week units in both middle and high school. Recreation directors, youth leaders, and youth ministers can pull out isolated activities or recreate the retreat experience.

Reviving the Wonder is organized around three important areas:

Part One: Optimum Learning Environments
The characteristics of a wonder-inspiring learning environment are approached from the five different modalities used to foster growth among youth: hope, humor, heroes, head, and heart.

Part Two: The Personal Journey
The journey to discover the wonder in life begins with an opening of the heart and a journey within to seek the inner self, to define beliefs and values, and to determine a mission in life.

Part Three: Transformations
Youth need to define themselves as male or female, and establish appropriate boundaries. They need to find meaningful ways of contributing to their family, their school, and their community. They need to know they are cared for, supported, and encouraged by their parents and teachers, and as they make the passage to adulthood, they need to be honored and celebrated by the community of adults.

Those who work with youth in all of the three areas will find the greatest success when they create programs based on a clear understanding of the heritage and culture of the youth with whom they are working. This is important work, and it takes enormous amounts of compassion and love. It is also very satisfying work when you realize that you have become a significant contributor to the empowerment of healthy young people.

Reviving the wonder in youth means resuscitating their hopes, dreams, and beliefs in a wonderful life journey. As adults, we become privileged to join these young people, to draw out their inner child, who once danced with abandonment and dreamed of limitless possibilities. Reviving the wonder in youth will encourage our children to be who they truly are — without shame. Masks are dropped, breathing goes deeper, and the true self comes forward without fear.

RIC STUECKER
LOUISVILLE, KENTUCKY

Acknowledgments

Suze and I want to thank the following for their contributions to our work and this book:

AT NATIONAL TRAINING ASSOCIATES, Wayne and Nancy for their constant help and support and belief in our work and their dedication to making it happen. To the NTA staff, especially Maggi and Lisa, who every day make our lives and travels easier. To Buzz for encouraging us to create new programs and to write this book.

To EMILY for her constant encouragement and final review of this material, and for taking care of us whenever we are working in San Mateo.

To LORNA at WordWrap for her brilliant editing and design work.

To THE STUDENTS who inspired us with their enthusiasm, creativity, brilliance, and spirit. Reviving the Wonder was created at the following school sites: Saint Bernard School (Louisville, KY), Saint Stephen Martyr School (Louisville, KY), Holy Cross High School (Louisville, KY), North Ridge High School (Middlebury, IN), El Molino High School (Forestville, CA), Hillsdale High School (San Mateo, CA), Burlingame High School (Burlingame, CA), Ceredo-Kenova High School (Ceredo, WV), and the West Virginia Teen Institute at Glenville State College (Glenville, WV).

PART ONE

Optimum Learning Environments

We came to the conclusion that mental health, happiness, and contentment is a natural state for human beings. We further concluded that this natural state is ever present, and available to each of us at every moment.

— ROGER MILLS

Youth need safe learning environments where relationships are built between adults and youth as well as among youth themselves; where individual learning styles are honored; where all youth are challenged to lead; where youth can imagine, hope, dream, design, create, and do. The characteristics of optimum, wonder-producing learning environments can be summarized using five words, as described in detail in the first five chapters: hope, humor, heroes, head, heart.

HOPE Classes and programs are future-oriented, see the future as hopeful and positive, and create communities within the learning space where staff and youth interact in ways that promote good citizenship. See Chapter 1.

HUMOR Laughter is common and natural. Play is incorporated into learning, games, and activities, which in turn become metaphors for significant concepts and ideas. Participants learn to breathe deeply and expand their thinking. See Chapter 2.

HEROES Adults see themselves as positive role models who inspire youth. Youth are encouraged to define personal leadership styles and use their leadership in real and significant situations. See Chapter 3.

HEAD Youth are presented challenges in ways that engage their individual learning styles and capacities. They are challenged to think critically, creatively, and collaboratively. See Chapter 4.

HEART Passionate learning occurs. Youth build character and create positive aspirations. See Chapter 5.

1   Hope

Hitch your wagon to a star.

— RALPH WALDO EMERSON

An environment that revives the wonder in youth is a place where all participants form a community of hope. A great teacher looks to the future with hope and courage, with confidence and optimism, and with spirit and wonder. Unfortunately, many learning environments (schools and communities, and the victims of those environments) are stuck in the present or look backward, toward the past. Teachers, kids, and their families are having problems in the present because they are looking to the past — as either a time when everything was better or a time containing the source of their problems. "We are as we are now because of what happened then" becomes their mantra. To revive the wonder in youth, the hoped-for future must be defined in positive terms and created as a realistic possibility.

Teach to a Hoped-For Future

When I was a new teacher, I met the poet and educator Charity James. Charity had come to this country from Great Britain at the invitation of the National Association of Independent Schools. Based on her experiences in schools on both sides of the Atlantic, Charity wrote *Young Lives at Stake*, a now-classic book in which a revolutionary approach to teaching young people is described.[1] Calling her method "individualized thinking and making" and "an enquiry approach," she challenges young people first to explore themselves and then to investigate their world and their relationship to that world. Through this approach, youth are taught to become effective citizens of the world and to make positive changes. Charity believes that all teachers must teach to their hoped-for future and create this hoped-for future in the lives of children.

Create a Community of Hope

One of the strongest cultural myths is that of the rugged individualist. However, as in the past, our survival into the future relies more on the interdependence of people working toward a common and inspiring goal than on the heroics of individual Daniel Boones.

At a time when competition includes winning at all cost and the resulting loss of integrity, creating collaborative communities in which individuals invest in each other's success is crucial. Communities of hope have the following characteristics:

- All individuals have the right to participate.

- All individuals are equal.

- Everyone takes his/her rightful place.

- Rights, responsibilities, and rules are created by the community and are fairly implemented.

- There is a positive mission.

- Individuals invest in each other's success.

- Group activities are noncompetitive and foster the mission of the community.

- Challenges are positive and future-oriented.

THE PROCESS OF BUILDING COMMUNITY can be fostered by following five stages of development:

1. Frame the activity.
2. Experience the activity.
3. Discuss the experience.
4. Generalize to the real world.
5. Inspire permission.

Circle of Life

When building a community of hope with youth, I like to begin with a birthday circle, also called a Circle of Life. Participants are asked to create a large circle around the room, in silence, using only nonverbal signals, and to find their place in the circle according to their birthdate. As a metaphor this circle represents the community of hope:

- Each person finds a place in the Circle of Life according to the accident of birth.

- Each person has a place equidistant from the center, equal to all others.

- Each person has an origin, a specific place to which they can always return.

- All people in the circle of life are responsible for the community's survival.

- All people have equal rights and responsibilities.

For a complete description of the Circle of Life, see page 93.

---

1. Frame the activity.

The teacher, facilitator, or group leader must present the group with a general understanding of the purpose of the activity or set of activities. This satisfies those in the group who feel they need to know why they are participating, what they will learn, and how this activity relates to the general scope, direction, and fundamental values of the program. The framing proceeds with an interplay of statements and questions. For example, you might say, "We are going to experience a series of team challenges and discover how we can work together to achieve specific goals." Then ask the following questions:

- Has anyone here ever played on a team or worked with a group trying to accomplish a specific task?

- What kind of team?

- What was fun about working or playing on a team?

- Was it always fun?

- Was the team successful?

- Has anyone here been on a team that won a lot of games, but you didn't have fun?

- What happened?

- Has anyone here been on a team where you seldom won but had a great time?

- How come?

- So in your experience, how do you define "team success"? What ingredients would you specify for making the experience fun? How could you insure that you and your teammates would be successful and still have a good time working and playing together?

2. Experience the activity.

The instructions should be clear, concise, and understood by all. Give the instructions step by step, one step at a time. To avoid confusion, do not give more than one instruction at a time.

If possible, use a small group of role models to show the larger group a sample of what they will be doing. This helps to give everyone a clear picture before they begin the activity. Give everyone an opportunity to ask questions for clarification. Repeat the questions when giving your response.

Ask for attention and wait until you get it (usually indicated by the silence of the group and all eyes focused on the facilitator) before you say, "Begin."

With some activities — especially where small-group discussion is a part of the activity or where each small group must finish a product at the same time

— give several warning signals. Example: "You have three minutes to finish," or, "How many groups need additional time? Okay, take three more minutes."

Bells with pleasing tones, chimes, or wooden train-type whistles work well to indicate "Stop." Police or coaching whistles are too harsh and tend to stimulate activity rather than indicate a cessation of activity.

3. Discuss the experience.

Discussion questions should be "open," allowing for a free flow of ideas and descriptions of experiences, rather than "closed," or seeking specific answers. I find a few simple questions that allow for a flow of thought work better than long sequences of questions seeking specific answers. Sample questions:

What did you experience? Can you describe what it was like for you? How might you describe it for someone who wasn't here?

What did you feel? Did anything scare you? Did you have to take a risk to participate? Was the risk worth it? Did you have fun? Were you let down? Did you take a risk and now you wish you hadn't?

What do you need to be able to take a risk? By taking this risk, did you learn something new?

What did you learn? Would you recommend this activity to others? Would you do it again at another time?

When someone expresses a feeling or describes an experience, ask if others in the group have had a similar experience. The discovery of experiences or feelings in common adds to group cohesion. For example, you might ask or say:

Who else here had an experience like John's?

Raise your hand if you had to take a risk to do this activity.

4. Generalize to the real world.

The group needs to understand that these activities are not isolated — that one activity relates to another and that each of the activities is a metaphor for real-world situations. Emphasize what is learned by doing the activity and lead the discussion portion of the activity to the application of what has been learned to real-world experiences. For example, ask questions like the following:

How is this like life?

Thinking about what you learned, where is a time and place in your life you could use these skills or understandings?

Where and how could you use this knowledge?

5. Inspire permission.

Permission is the group level at which the most learning occurs. The leader or teacher knows this level has been reached when the group enthusiastically takes risks. Everything flows smoothly from activity to activity. There is little or no resistance. Laughter flows freely. The laughter is natural and comes from the joy of participation — never at the expense of others or from nervousness or reluctance to participate.

The leader can "read" the group for permission by noticing and interpreting the *breathing* of the group.

> When the breathing of the group is *low* (literally low in the chest and down to the belly) and effortless, there is high permission and high performance. When individuals and groups are breathing low, they hear well, they think effectively and with reason and depth, and they respond easily to instructions and/or questions. If permission is high (and breathing is low), participants' bodies are relaxed and fluid, words come easily, thoughts expressed show reflection, and the group is willing to ask additional questions and make additional comments.

> When the breathing of a group is *high* (literally high in the chest up to the throat, like a pant) there is little permission. Performance is spotty. Participants have trouble hearing the leader and are slow to join in; they answer questions in single words or short phrases that reflect little thought. Groups merely "go through the motions" or even exhibit a reluctance to follow instructions. Discussions are short and reveal a shallowness of thought and a reluctance to answer questions. When permission is really low, the leader may see the bodies of participants become rigid or assume a fight-or-flight mode.

Reading breathing is the single most effective way a leader can determine his or her relationship with the group, the level of safety created, how much rapport has been established, and whether participants are ready for more risky behaviors (and more learning). When a group comes to a place where breathing stops, the leader must win greater permission before proceeding — by going back to less risky activities and attempting to increase permission with the group.

HERE ARE SOME WAYS to try to increase permission:

- Move slower.

- Discuss each activity and show its purpose.

- Encourage natural leaders in the group to "buy into" the activities with greater gusto and enthusiasm, thus role-modeling for the others.

- Stop everything and discuss with the group what they perceive as roadblocks or barriers.
- Negotiate — get the group to try a low-risk activity, then discuss it before moving to a higher-risk activity.

When the group stops breathing, the participants no longer feel safe. The cycle of establishing safety, building rapport, and inspiring permission must begin again. This process of inspiring permission can be broken down into three distinct stages: I, We, and Task.

The I Stage

The I Stage is marked by each individual's concern with personal safety and comfort. For example, when entering a class or workshop for the first time, most people look for someone they know to sit with. They examine the room for comfortable furniture and seek out refreshments. They look over any written material, find a place for their things, wonder if they will learn anything, and review the schedule to discover breaks, lunch, and dismissal. In all these actions, the major concerns are safety and personal comfort.

In the process of community building, the I Stage is called *forming*. As the group or community forms, personal considerations become less important and individuals begin to feel more and more a part of the larger community.

The We Stage

Moving from I to We takes some time and effort. The process can be facilitated through the use of team-building activities, the establishment of a group mission, and the development of specific processes and procedures the group will use.

Within the context of community building, this is called *norming*. Individual rights and responsibilities are examined, and out of this context rules are created. Three crucial rules are encouraged at Reviving the Wonder retreats and in Reviving the Wonder classrooms; these are also excellent life rules. (See "Three Crucial Rules" on page 9.) These three rules for living are summarized in the following Chinese proverb:[2]

> *If there is light in the soul*
> *There will be beauty in the person.*
> *If there is beauty in the person,*
> *There will be harmony in the house.*
> *If there is harmony in the house,*
> *There will be order in the nation.*
> *If there is order in the nation,*
> *There will be peace in the world.*

Three Crucial Rules

Rule One: Take care of yourself.

In life as in any classroom or at any training event, taking care of oneself is very important. Encourage participants to participate, learn, and be good citizens. Youth need to be reminded that each individual is his/her own best friend and responsible for his/her actions. This includes the following instructions:

Listen. Listen to the leader and know what to do. If you are sitting next to someone who disturbs your listening, get up and move. Do not interfere with others' listening.

Participate with enthusiasm. Only you can determine the amount of energy you are willing to give to an activity. When you participate with enthusiasm, you inspire others to do likewise.

Engage with the group. You can decide to be a positive part of the group or to isolate yourself. Invest in the success of your group.

Kids like to say, "I'm so bored! Bored, bored, bored! When is someone or something going to entertain me?" Human beings are all creative geniuses and those who claim to be bored are probably refusing to look around and find something interesting to examine, study, read, create, or do. Each person needs to take responsibility for leading him/herself out of boredom and into excitement, out of trouble or into it. Each individual can engage in actions that enrich and empower his/her own life and the lives of others, or conversely each individual can engage in actions that limit his/her mission and potential to make life compelling. The full meaning of Rule One is that each person is solely responsible for him/herself and the consequences to his/her actions, as well as for the amount and quality of the energy that is brought to everyday living.

Rule Two: Take care of each other.

Successful living depends upon social alliances among individuals and within groups. When people take care of each other, then the group as a whole succeeds. Much more can be accomplished as a group than as an individual, and the joy of succeeding is also shared with family and friends. Encourage youth to support each other and invest in each other's successes, especially when working in groups.

- Make sure everyone has the opportunity to participate.
- Welcome each other into groups.
- Stay positive.
- Don't belittle or put down others.

Rule Three: Take care of this place.

Take care of the room where we are working, our homes, our communities, our neighborhoods, our city, our country, our planet. My grandfather used to tell me that if each of us were to sweep in front our own house, soon the whole city, the whole state, the whole country, and the whole world would be clean. Likewise, if each of us takes care of ourselves and our responsibilities, if we connect with others in positive ways, and if we individually and in groups form missions of harmony and peace — and act on these missions — we become stewards of our lives, our communities, and our planet. In the classroom or retreat setting, begin by encouraging participants to do the following:

Take ownership of this area.
It belongs to you as much as it belongs to the facilitators, the adult leaders, and the other participants.

Respect the materials you are given.
Take care of the color markers, pencils, paper, and any other materials or equipment you are given. Put them away at the end of the activity.

Help each other clean up.
Clean up spills as soon as they are made. Clean up your work area after each activity.

ANOTHER IMPORTANT PART of the norming stage is the creation of a common mission. The leader must bring the group to an understanding of its mission, from the fundamental principles of the learning experience to the ultimate goals of the tasks set by the group. The five concepts expressed in the five chapters within Part One can be used as the guiding principles for the Reviving the Wonder group experience and as a way to lead young people to an understanding of their mission and the goals of the group experience:

Hope Today in this room we hope to create a community where everyone will be honored, all ideas will be treated with respect, all will participate, and no one will feel left out, put down, or diminished.

Humor Today we will be free to laugh and play and create. We will learn by playing games and doing activities. Each of the activities has a purpose; each of the games is a metaphor for life and how we hope to live it.

Heroes The leaders in this room are our heroes. They have stepped forward into a leadership role, for which they should be honored. They have stated by their actions that they will be role models. All the people in this room will have an opportunity to examine their leadership style and capacity. At the end of this experience, everyone will be able to use these leadership skills by performing service in our communities.

Head To create this community of hope, we think — both as individuals and as a group. The result will be solutions that are useful as well as creative.

Heart We will inspire ourselves and each other. We will work with passion and courage. We will create a community of hope here, today, in this space, and when we leave we will seek to re-create it in our lives.

The Task Stage

During the final stage, because the group is bonded and feeling safe, it now performs at high levels. This is called the *performing* or task stage. Tasks move smoothly and with high energy and enthusiasm the group easily takes on new challenges.

This is the stage all facilitators and teachers seek for the groups they lead. Here tasks are fun and everyone dances on each other's energy and good spirits. It is here that retreats, workshops, and transformative experiences reach the peak of their magic — and therefore become memorable. Thus the learning that took place during the retreat is more likely to be remembered and used. There's a greater probability that participants will therefore apply their learning to the real world.

Checklist for Empowering Hope
in a Learning Environment

How many of the following questions can you answer with an unqualified "yes"?

_____ I ask youth to think about a positive future.

_____ I dream, and I promote dreaming and daydreaming in others.

_____ I have a personal mission statement, and I ask all youth to develop a personal mission statement that includes a hoped-for personal future and possible contributions to society.

_____ I consider the entire range of individual learning styles and capacities when I plan activities so that everyone can participate.

_____ I use activities that are collaborative rather than competitive.

_____ I involve the group in collaborative rule making.

_____ I value the opinions of all youth in my program.

_____ I encourage youth to invest in each other's success.

_____ I promote leadership positions for all the youth in my program.

_____ I plan activities that group youth with those who may not be in their tight friendship circle.

_____ I encourage youth to discover and value the talents of those who are not their usual friends.

_____ I continuously teach youth to encourage each other and to eliminate put-downs.

_____ I create an environment where youth will feel a sense of community.

_____ When conflicts arise, I encourage students to peacefully resolve them.

_____ I empower youth by teaching conflict resolution strategies and consensus decision making.

_____ I establish reliable norms and procedures everyone can trust.

_____ Through team-building activities, I create high energy and enthusiasm for learning and the completion of tasks.

Resources

This manual includes many team-building activities. See especially the activities in Chapter 9, "Connecting with Others." The following books are also useful resources for building a community of hope in the learning environment.

Bodine, Richard J., Donna K. Crawford, and Fred Schrumpf. *Creating the Peaceable School: A Comprehensive Program for Teaching Conflict Resolution.* Champaign, IL: Research Press, 1994.

Karns, Michelle. *Ethnic Barriers and Biases: How to Become an Agent for Change.* Sebastopol, CA: National Training Associates, 1998.

Quiroz, Hilda Clarice. *Start with the Kids: 5 Days to Building a Classroom Community.* Santa Cruz, CA: Education Training and Research Associates, 1997.

2   Humor

Laughter is the shortest distance between two people.
— VICTOR BORGE

Other than human touch, laughter most quickly releases endorphins (natural chemicals that allow us to experience good feelings). Laughter promotes deep, healthy breathing. Deep breathing and the release of endorphins are directly related to deep thinking and creativity. Students who laugh, play, and breathe deeply think more creatively and create new, interesting, and effective solutions to the challenges presented to them. Classes where humor is honored produce students who score higher on academic tests. Humor and play are crucial to reviving the wonder in youth.

Great thinking and learning is built on humor and play. Albert Einstein played with ideas all his life. To be a genius is to play with the same variables all of us see, but to be able to view them in relation to each other in new and different ways.

Laughter in Treatment

Some years ago I had the honor of managing a treatment center that served chemically dependent adolescents. What immediately struck me was how seldom the kids laughed, and when they did laugh it was invariably at others. This in turn resulted in anger, violence, and fighting. When this same group of kids met with the recreational therapist, they either didn't know how to play or refused to play and enjoy themselves in a light-hearted manner. Risk taking in positive ways was too dangerous for them.

We knew we were reaching the kids (that is, our therapeutic methods were working) when finally they could openly laugh, freely, and deeply at themselves and their situations. At the same time, they were letting go of the cruel laughter they had exhibited early in their treatment. In addition, those who let themselves laugh and play became more flexible in their thinking, more positive in their behavior, and more likely to be successful in their lifestyle changes.

Approaching problem-solving with humor can build a foundation of persistence. After a series of failed experiments, Thomas Edison said: "We haven't failed. We now know a thousand things that won't work, so we are much closer to finding what will."[1]

I often ask participants direct questions about their experience with humor and play. (See "Discussion Starters" below.) Whenever and wherever I ask these questions, the audience begins to twitter, then chuckle, then laugh quietly, then laugh out loud, then guffaw. People in the audience look at each other, see if laughing is okay, start shaking their heads — "Yes, I've done that too!" — and finally let go as they recognize a truth in themselves and in others.

Comedian Jerry Lewis puts it something like this: "If I slip on a banana peel, it's a tragedy. If I see you slip on a banana peel, that's comedy." At its deepest level, tragedy and comedy intermix to create the human comedy, in which reside both sadness and grief. Survival comes with laughter.

With humor and play, we can all reach back into childhood and become younger. And becoming younger (at least in spirit!) we become healthier. Roger Mills, who has had great success throughout the United States helping both individuals and communities in the deepest despair turn their lives and neighborhoods around, has built his Health Realization model on this idea:[2]

It then occurred to us that children, especially very young children, also tend to act in happy, healthy ways. They have few self-esteem problems and seem

---

Discussion Starters

Questions About Humor

Do you laugh?

Do you laugh often?

Do you laugh out loud?

Have you noticed how everyone has a distinctive and distinctively funny laugh?

Have you ever laughed so hard you fell over?

Have you ever laughed so hard you got dizzy?

Have you ever laughed so hard you forgot where you were?

Have you ever laughed while drinking and then snorted liquid out your nose?

Have you ever laughed so hard you nearly peed in your pants? Did you pee in your pants?

Have you ever laughed so long you forgot what you were laughing at? You just got into the pleasure of laughing?

Have you ever laughed so long it was hard to stop?

Have you ever laughed until your stomach muscles hurt? Until you could no longer get your breath?

Have you ever laughed so hard that all of a sudden everything seemed funny?

Questions About Play

Do you sing in the shower?

Have you ever been singing or rapping in the shower and the reverberation made you sound so good you thought you might consider a recording contract?

Have you ever cranked up the car windows and turned up the sound system real loud, then sung with the tunes?

Have you ever locked your bedroom door, cranked up the tunes, and danced like a rock star? Have you ever done this in your underwear?

Have you ever looked in the mirror, said "Hi there, gorgeous!" and kissed yourself?

Have you rolled on the grass lately?

naturally motivated. Small children master the highly complicated tasks of walking and talking with minimum prodding from adults. Children also get upset from time to time, but they quickly rebound. They don't hold grudges. They don't relive the past or fret about the future. Most children live in the present moment. Because children seem to live naturally in mental health and because we discovered adults who seemed to have rediscovered this same mental health, we began to see that this mental health never really disappears — and is actually available to all humans when we begin to turn back to it. We came to the conclusion that mental health, happiness, and contentment [are] a natural state for human beings. We further concluded that this natural state is ever present, and available to each of us at every moment.

Humor and play take us immediately into that "present moment," allow us to drop our anxieties and our personal "masks," and take us into this natural mental health. Humor is the place where people connect with each other at their most human level. Is it surprising that resilient youth have been shown to have great senses of humor, laugh often, and know how to play?

HERE ARE SOME CHARACTERISTICS of learning environments where humor and play are honored:

1. It's safe to play.

Sarcasm and put-downs are never allowed. The quickest way to destroy a positive and exciting learning environment is to make (or allow others to make) sarcastic remarks to particular people about how they are performing. Same with put-downs. Neither verbal nor nonverbal put-downs should go unchallenged.

2. The activity is positively framed.

The trainer, teacher, or facilitator always takes the game or activity seriously, bringing great energy and enthusiasm to the play. The game or activity is seen as crucial to learning. A great facilitator presents the activity as the most important event in the world in the present moment.

3. The activity is related to concepts and skills the learners need.

In discussing what is experienced during the activity, the facilitator leads the group to conclusions, showing how the skill or concept is useful in the real world. The facilitator asks questions such as "How useful is what you have just learned?" "Where could you use this skill?" "Is life ever like this?" "Do you ever feel like this at other times?"

4. Activities are sequenced from low risk to high risk.

The adult leader must choose activities appropriate to the group, beginning with low risk. When you see participants literally stop breathing, their bodies stiffen, and their reluctance or refusal to participate, then you know they have been taken beyond their level of trust and permission. By building from success to success and pointing out how successful they have been in previous activities, a facilitator is able to move players to higher risks and more learning.

5. Games and humor are not a special occasion.

Humor, play, games, and learning activities are common, everyday occurrences. They are valued as a method of learning, not saved up just for special occasions.

6. Playing the game is not a reward for good behavior.

Play is serious learning business — not a reward for doing "more serious" work. Threatening young people with isolation from a game or fun activity destroys the whole learning environment.

Resources

The following books are recommended resources for implementing humor into a learning environment.

Karns, Michelle. *How to Create Positive Relationships with Students: A Handbook of Group Activities and Teaching Strategies.* Champaign, IL: Research Press, 1994.

Roehlkepartain, Jolene L. *Building Assets Together: 135 Group Activities for Helping Youth Succeed.* Minneapolis, MN: Search Institute, 1995.

Checklist for Promoting Humor in a Learning Environment

How many of the following questions can you answer with an unqualified "yes"?

_____ I laugh often, freely, and deeply.

_____ I laugh at myself and at humorous situations.

_____ In my program, I create an environment in which it is safe to laugh and play.

_____ I believe that having fun, laughing, and playing are essential in my program.

_____ In my program, youth laugh often, freely, and deeply.

_____ I create and use learning games to teach positive concepts.

_____ I try to engage and motivate learners who appear bored.

_____ I model high energy, enthusiasm, curiosity, and joy.

_____ I encourage youth to be themselves.

---

3   Heroes

It is the responsibility of every adult — especially parents, educators, and religious leaders — to make sure that children hear what we have learned from the lessons of life, and to hear over and over that we love them and that they are not alone.

— MARIAN WRIGHT EDELMAN

When I was a young boy, my father put a padlock on the door to his basement workshop. His workshop was so spotless you could eat off the floor. On the wall were outlines of all his tools, allowing him to easily find them when they were needed and put them away when he was done using them. Nails, screws, and other hardware essentials were kept in labeled jars that were arranged by size and color. I could destroy the perfect order of my dad's workshop world in less than five minutes.

I honor my father. Because of his presence in my life, I get to appointments on time, with everything I need inside my briefcase. I set high standards for my work. But everything I know about using tools comes from my grandfather, who worked as a hardwood refinisher and general carpenter. In my memory, I can still hear him, see him, and smell him. I can smell his pipe, the wood, and the lacquers, paint, and varnishes. Grandpa found his tools just by reaching out for them. He always let me into his workshop, and while I watched him work or helped him, we talked about life, and he always answered my questions.

I honor my grandfather. Because of his presence in my life I know how to build relationships with kids.

All youth need a variety of high quality relationships with adults who care about them — at home, in their schools, and in their neighborhood. They need adults like my father and my grandfather, who are willing to take the time to listen, advise, instruct, model values and standards, and just be there for help and support.

For the past twenty years, researchers in the area of youth resiliency have focused on the importance of relationships between caring adults and youth within positive learning environments. This was also revealed in the work of Peter Benson and the Search Institute as they developed a list of developmental assets shown to promote healthy youth. In his now classic work *The Troubled Journey*, Benson writes:[1]

> *Positive development requires constant exposure to interlocking systems of support, control, and structure. In the ideal, young people — via schools, families, community organizations, and religious institutions — constantly interact with caring principled adults. These patterns of support, control and structure function as external assets, providing young people with webs of safety and love important for stimulating and nurturing healthy development.*
>
> *Adolescence is the bridge between a childhood surrounded by networks of external assets, and adulthood, in which these networks are partially supplanted by the internal checks and balances that enable the individual to make wise choices when beyond the reach of childhood's protective cocoon. It is of primary importance, then, to nourish — particularly during adolescence — a range of internal assets. They are the commitments, values, and competencies that help an individual thrive competently and responsibly when "on one's own."*

The most recent generation of youth looks at each other as their role models and at media figures as their heroes. Russell Quaglia, director of the National Center for Student Aspirations, reports on the results of research in *Believing in Achieving*.[2]

> *In a study conducted by the National Center for Student Aspirations surveying almost 8,000 high school students around the country, less than half said they admire and respect their teachers, and even less saw their teachers as role models....*
>
> *Why do so many of our students consider tycoons, fleetingly beautiful media stars and even obscene cartoon characters as the standard of success? What have we as parents, educators and a society done or not done to allow this to happen? What about heroes who look like you and me? What about heroes who work in schools? Well, what about it?*
>
> *Here's the bottom line. We all have to shape up and realize that being a hero is much more than making a public pronouncement. It is taking on a huge responsibility.... We must realize that being a hero and a mentor can and should be perceived as synonymous.*

Indeed, if we as adults are to be heroes and mentors, we must first look at *how* we communicate with and manage youth. It is very easy for us to *tell* kids what to do rather than *show* them through our personal modeling. It is very easy for us to take a power stance when managing youth — ordering them about, raising our voices, using our power as adults — and provoking a power struggle with them rather than working with them as partners. In those situations, we often lose youth, especially high-risk youth, even when we might in the moment win the power struggle. We often find it easier to construct service projects where youth provide the labor and adults provide the leadership in both the design and implementation of the project. Actually, we need to let them discover their personal leadership potential by encouraging them to take responsibility for projects they design and are therefore meaningful to them. When we provide leadership how do youth learn to be leaders?

IN LEARNING ENVIRONMENTS that revive the wonder in youth:

> **Adults use influence rather than power.** They are heroes who build relationships of influence rather than relationships based on power. This way, these everyday heroes become role models; youth choose to connect with them, and choose to emulate their skills, attitudes, and behaviors.

> **Adults promote leadership.** They help youth understand their leadership potential and promote the leadership roles of all youth — in the school and in the community.

> **Adults create meaningful opportunities for service.** They help youth accept responsible positions as mentors and in other service positions where the work is of significant value to others.

Use Influence Rather Than Power

Most of us, as adults, tend to use our power over youth when we are managing them in learning situations. As Michael Grinder has written in *ENVoY: A Personal Guide to Classroom Management,* "We are inadvertently in love with the Influence of Power, and we need to be in love with the Power of Influence."[3] We tend to shame and blame when our students make mistakes. We tend to raise our voices and order them to do what we want. We tend to remind them we are the adults and in charge of operations. We often act like military leaders commanding the troops. When we take these stances — especially with youth who are "in trouble" or "inappropriate" — we destroy (or fail to build) positive relationships. With the at-risk population, in particular, that is with those we most want to help and those who most need our help, rules and structures and power will not work until we have created a relationship of influence.

In the table on page 20, you can see the differences between operating from a position of power and operating from a position of influence.

Mentoring for Youth

Heroes and mentors of influence are able to do the following:

- Accept their roles as mentors, advocates, and teachers of youth with confidence and with ease

- Use their natural power over youth only when needed (for example, to get attention) and then gracefully move to influence and relationship

Characteristics of Power	Characteristics of Influence
Is external — as when an adult tells a kid what to do	Is internal — youth learn internal locus of control
Provokes win-lose situations	Promotes win-win situation
Is short in duration	Is long-lasting
Loses efficacy when used too often	Is highly effective over time
Threatens the relationship between adults and youth	Maintains the relationship between adults and youth

- Trust youth, and empower youth to believe in themselves
- Focus first on youth and their needs, rather than focusing on their own convenience or personal needs
- Listen to youth — and respond to what is heard as a way of promoting meaningful dialogue that focuses on the understanding and opinion of youth
- Use their personal experiences as a source of wisdom, to enrich and inform — and refrain from telling war stories or using personal self-disclosure to impress
- Tell the truth
- Express their feelings using a feeling language and encourage youth to do the same
- Understand that youth may view life differently, and allow youth to express their distinctive opinions and understandings
- Use voice tones, body language, and eye contact that promote relationship and influence rather than power and control

Promote Leadership

All kids have a role to play in leadership. Often adults have a desire to define a certain group as the "leadership group" — for their physical attractiveness, athletic grace, charm, wit, willingness to please adults, or perceived intelligence — and then promote their leadership by giving them roles, sending them to workshops, and letting them represent the school to others. I applaud these leadership groups for using their talents, but in the community of hope everybody has a responsibility to lead and to take responsibility for the necessary tasks that maintain the community.

Quite often Reviving the Wonder events are held on Saturdays, usually at the same time as the infamous "Saturday school." (You may recall Saturday from the film *The Breakfast Club,* during which errant youth must spend most of Saturday doing meaningless assignments or performing chores around the school for transgressions such as failing to complete homework or being late to class.) I generally ask the site coordinator to allow the Saturday school kids to come to our Reviving the Wonder retreat as an alternative. On a number of occasions, I have confused the Saturday school group with the youth leadership group — it's quite easy for me to confuse "class leaders" with those often labeled "class losers" as they often dress alike, especially on weekends. In almost every case this has happened, the adults have had the opportunity to see the Saturday school students in a completely different way, and in nearly every case the Saturday school kids have shined as leaders.

My colleague and mentor, Raymond Golarz, often tells the story of the mixup of John T. and John P. He also recounts this story in *The Power of Participation*.[4]

> *Several years ago, students identified by the district as promising young leaders were invited to spend an all-expenses-paid weekend at Notre Dame University, participating in a youth leadership training program. One year there were two students whose names were very similar — John P. Williams and John T. Williams. John T. was a member of the National Honor Society and had an outstanding curricular and extra-curricular record during his first two years of high school. John P., on the other hand, was categorically defined as learning disabled. Although he attended school regularly, he did not excel academically and never participated in extra-curricular activities.*
>
> *Through a clerical error, John P. Williams received the written invitation to the leadership program, and he decided to attend. (The error was not noticed until after the students returned from the program.) Several weeks later, the building principal complimented his staff, particularly on the selection of John Williams. He had been advised by Notre Dame that John showed the leadership qualities that those conducting the workshop truly admired. I am confident that John P. Williams responded at Notre Dame according to his understanding of their collective perception of what they thought he was. In fact, they created a new reality for John P.*

When given the opportunity, students who do not shine when performing the traditional tasks of school quite often show amazing intelligence, creativity, and leadership aptitude. In fact, more often than not, the television series *Biography* chronicles the lives of famous people who led outstanding lives that broke the mold, successful people who took the less traveled path. Sometimes, the John P.'s and the Saturday School kids grow up to make real and lasting contributions to our world.

Adult leadership is not simply organizing and commanding others. Groups attempting to complete complicated tasks require other kinds of leadership skills. Creative problem solving requires leaders who can visualize new answers. A thorough understanding of the process of implementation that will function best is the key to the development of new ideas. When engaged in problem solving over a long period of time, groups need mediators who can ease tensions and negotiate common ground when team members disagree. The activities in this book are designed to encourage all students to discover and use their individual leadership style.

Varying Leadership Styles

Everyone has a different leadership style. Adults who support a learning environment help each young person discover his or her own leadership style.

EFFECTIVE GROUPS NEED the four following types of leaders:

Task focused

Leaders who run meetings, encourage movement toward a goal, are action oriented, and make sure things get done

Process focused

Leaders who figure out how a goal can be reached

Mediation focused

Leaders who keep the process going, keep up the group's energy, and mediate conflicts

Vision focused

Leaders who see the big picture and keep the group focused on the ultimate goal

Create Opportunities for Service

Schools can be excellent places to foster service that makes a difference. At one of my schools, every kid is in a mentoring relationship over time. Fifth graders are matched with first graders, sixth with second, seventh with third, and eighth with fourth. A student task force designs special events. Some students become peer mentors, some become peer tutors, and some become peer mediators.

Through these service opportunities, students often reflect on their own experiences and change their behaviors. Sometimes older students are paired with younger students who exhibit the same difficulties. The process of mentoring the younger students help the older ones solve their own problems. Peer tutors become better students and organize their time more efficiently. Peer mediators learn to control their own anger and experience fewer conflicts. These cross-grade experiences end up turning the entire school district into a community of hope.

HERE ARE SOME SUGGESTIONS for making sure service programs are meaningful to the participants:

- Involve youth in the design of the program, including making contacts with community agencies and creating/coordinating the projects.

- Make sure all youth have the opportunity to participate.

- Ask youth to reflect on their experiences by keeping a journal and attending group discussions.

- Ask youth to evaluate their service experiences and their value to the program.

- Celebrate the experience and honor participants.

Checklist for Promoting Heroes in a Learning Environment

How many of the following questions can you answer with an unqualified "yes"?

____ I see myself as an advisor, mentor, and advocate for youth.

____ All youth are seen and used as leaders.

____ Youth take on leadership positions throughout my program.

____ I challenge both boys and girls to be leaders.

____ I ask youth to reflect upon their leadership and efficacy in group projects.

____ I help youth become mentors, tutors, and mediators to younger children.

____ I ensure that youth are offered the opportunity to do meaningful work.

____ I know the youth in my program and they know me.

____ I support students in their search for success.

____ I listen more than I tell.

____ I have frequent and meaningful conversations with youth.

____ I set high standards for youth and provide the support they need to meet these challenges.

____ I help youth identify with positive role models, including both people they know directly and those they encounter in the media.

Resources

The following books are recommended resources for developing and implementing meaningful mentoring and service learning projects for youth.

Crockett, Lib, and Jay Smink. *The Mentoring Guidebook: A Practical Manual for Designing and Managing a Mentoring Program.* Clemson, SC: National Dropout Prevention Center, 1991.

Goldberg, Mark F. *How to Design an Advisory System for a Secondary School.* Alexandria, VA: Association for Supervision and Curriculum Development, 1998.

Karns, Michelle. *DOisms: Ten Prosocial Principles That Ensure Caring Connections with Kids.* Sebastopol, CA: National Training Associates, 1995.

Lewis, Barbara A., and Pamela Espeland. *The Kid's Guide to Service Projects: Over 500 Service Ideas for Young People Who Want to Make a Difference.* Minneapolis, MN: Free Spirit Publishing, 1995.

Lewis, Barbara A., Pamela Espeland, and Caryn Pernu. *The Kid's Guide to Social Action: How to Solve the Social Problems You Choose — and Turn Creative Thinking into Positive Action.* Minneapolis, MN: Free Spirit Publishing, 1998.

Witmer, Judith T., and Carolyn S. Anderson. *How to Establish a High School Service Learning Program.* Alexandria, VA: Association for Supervision and Curriculum Development, 1994.

4　Head

A man who has no imagination has no wings.

— MUHAMMAD ALI

I often ask students if they like to think. A few raise their hands. Then I ask them if thinking hurts their heads. More hands go up. Then I ask them if they think they are smart. Primary groups all enthusiastically raise their hands; they can't get their hands high enough. About half of a group of middle school students raise their hands, but with much less enthusiasm. High school students usually turn and point to one or two people they think are smart, and often those identified blush and are embarrassed. Finally I suggest that all of them are smart — geniuses, in fact — and they look at me like I'm crazy. I can almost hear some say, "Yeah, sure." Others just giggle.

I suggest that by just using 5 percent more brain capacity, they would be as smart as Einstein. And I tell them that Albert Einstein and Thomas Edison, if they had been tested for ADD and ADHD, very likely would have been considered learning disabled. (ADD, Attention Deficit Disorder, is considered a learning disability where a student has great difficulty staying focused on a task. These students are sometimes found "daydreaming," or unable to follow a logical sequence of learning events over time. When students are also observed to be hyperactive — unable to sit still for more than ten or fifteen minutes — they are considered to have ADHD, Attention Deficit with Hyperactivity Disorder.) I explain that there are many kinds of intelligence, many kinds of "smarts," and that all kinds of "heads" are needed if we are to find solutions to our personal problems and make improvements in our society.

Learning environments that revive the wonder in youth challenge young people to use their heads. How each individual uses his or her head depends on how each processes information, on a particular and unique set of capacities or "intelligences." Activities in a learning community engage both the left and right brain, as well as a variety of learning styles.

CONSIDER THE CHALLENGES facing those who work with youth today:

- Some scientists believe children born now may live from 90 to 130 years. During their lifetime they may have as many as five to eight careers.

- Observers believe we have moved from an industrial to an information age during which ideas can be products and those who work with new ideas, concepts, and solutions will be the most successful.

- Human knowledge is considered to double every eighteen months, and that time is quickly becoming shorter.

Those of us who are preparing youth to face the challenges of the future take on the task of helping them develop their individual genius in ways that will foster individual contributions. To meet these challenges, as youth become adults they will have to use a myriad of talents. Recent advances in brain research offer new directions and opportunities to develop capacities and "intelligences" in new ways.

Here are two models I find useful to understand how to challenge kids to use their heads:

Seven Kinds of Smart, from Thomas Armstrong, who applied Howard Gardner's theory of multiple intelligences to the school, home, and everyday life.

Three Distinctive Learning Styles, a model developed by Michael Grinder and described in his book *Righting the Educational Conveyor Belt*. This model suggest the ways human beings process, store, and use information.

Seven Kinds of Smart

As delineated by Thomas Armstrong in *Multiple Intelligences in the Classroom,* each of us is a combination of capacities, with our own unique set of strengths and weaknesses.[1]

Left Brain Smarts

Word Smart
People who are "word smart" often remember passages from famous poems, speeches, and literary works. They use words easily and skillfully, finding exact and creative ways of using and joining words and phrases for meaning and effect. They understand nuance and are sensitive to how words sound.

Some "word smart" people include William Shakespeare, Miguel Cervantes, Robert Frost, Saul Bellow, Hans Christian Andersen, Ernest Hemingway.

"Word smart" people might become novelists, playwrights, copy writers, editors, publishers, English teachers.

Number Smart

People who are "number smart" are able to solve mathematical and logical problems. They can discern logical or numerical patterns. They think through complex problems in a step-by-step method and value the beauty of process.

Some "number smart" people include Albert Einstein, Pythagoras, Sir Isaac Newton, Charles Darwin, Euclid.

"Number smart" people often become engineers, scientists in many fields, and teachers of mathematics and science.

Right Brain Smarts

Space Smart

People who are "space smart" understand how objects can be balanced, how colors work with one another, and how the size and shape of objects relate in space. They can manipulate the variables of color, size, and shape of objects and space in ways that are aesthetically appealing and meaningful.

Some "space smart" people include: Pablo Picasso, Leonardo da Vinci, Orson Welles, Frank Lloyd Wright.

"Space smart" people might become artists, photographers, sculptors, architects, movie directors, stage directors, interior designers, scenic designers for movies or stage, commercial artists, graphic designers, and teachers of visual arts.

Body Smart

People who are "body smart" are agile, flexible, graceful, athletic, in high control of their body movements, and can easily use and manipulate objects.

Some "body smart" people include Twyla Tharp, Joe Montana, Michael Jordan and Mikail Baryshnikov, Chris Evert, Sabrina and Venus Williams, Ginger Rogers.

"Body Smart" people often become professional athletes, dancers, entertainers, actors, coaches, and teachers of performing arts.

Music Smart

People who are "music smart" understand the makeup of music including sound, tone, timbre, and pitch. They can either create and perform music or have a special appreciation of musical expressiveness.

Some "music smart" people include Cole Porter, Irving Berlin, Stephen Sondheim, George and Ira Gershwin, John Lennon and Paul McCartney, Paul Simon, Johann Sebastian Bach, Wolfgang Amadeus Mozart, Aaron Copeland, Leonard Bernstein, Barbra Streisand, Ella Fitzgerald.

"Music smart" people often become musicians, composers, conductors, arrangers, music critics, disc jockeys, singers, rappers, entertainers.

People Smart	People who are "people smart" are able to discern, understand, and respond to other people — especially their moods, motivations, temperaments, and desires.
	Some "people smart" people include Sigmund Freud, Carl Jung, William Faulkner, F. Scott Fitzgerald, Oprah Winfrey, Rosie O'Donnell, Katie Couric.
	"People smart" people often become psychologists, novelists, interviewers, reporters, journalists, sales people, teachers.
Self Smart	People who are "self smart" understand themselves extremely well, especially their inner feelings, wants and desires, emotions, and personal strengths and weaknesses.
	Some "self smart" people include Buddha, Stephen Covey, John Keats, William Wordsworth, Marianne Moore.
	"Self smart" people often become psychologists, writers, poets, and artists.

Three Distinctive Learning Styles

Michael Grinder's model sees students as processing information in three distinctive learning styles: kinesthetic, auditory, and visual.[2]

Kinesthetic Learners

- Are physically oriented
- Move a lot
- Memorize by walking through it
- Touch people and stand close
- Point when reading
- Gesture often
- Respond physically
- Respect relationships more than rules
- Learn by doing

Kinesthetic learners need help with organization, systems, routines, and rules. Effective teaching strategies with kinesthetic learners include games, stories, metaphors, projects, demonstrations, props, movement, drama, small groups.

Auditory Learners

- Speak in rhythmic patterns
- Sometimes speak out
- Love to hear their own voices

- Move lips when reading
- Can mimic tone, timbre, and pitch
- Tell stories often
- Love hearing stories
- Memorize by steps, procedure, and sequence
- Learn by listening

Auditory learners need help with math, logic, and writing. Effective teaching strategies with auditory learners include stories, discussion, music, rhythms, rhymes, echo learning.

Visual Learners

- Are organized
- Are considered "scholars"
- Are good readers and spellers
- Follow with their eyes
- Observe everything
- Are neat and orderly
- Memorize by seeing pictures
- Learn by watching

Visual learners need help with play, movement, cooperative learning, and relationships. Effective teaching strategies for visual learners include logical presentations, lectures, reading, and seatwork.

In an educational setting, kinesthetic and auditory learners, who are most at risk of failing, are usually highly intelligent in the right-brain "intelligences." Visual learners are usually highly intelligent in the left-brain "intelligences." In most schools the left-brain visual students receive all the honors and awards. Most of the teaching is also designed for their learning style because most of the testing, especially as students become older, measures left-brain intelligence and visual learning. In fact, the entire culture of traditional schooling is based on left-brain intelligence and a visual learning style. As a result, right-brain students, kinesthetic learners, and auditory learners often find themselves "out of culture."

To engage the curiosity and imagination of all the learners, learning needs to be inquiry and discovery based. In a learning environment that revives the wonder in youth, big questions are asked and preparations are made for long and arduous voyages of discovery. The answers to these big questions are often larger than the knowledge of both students and teachers, and the voyages' destinations are sometimes unknown. The learning, in fact, is out of control — but the students are not. Learning becomes a bold adventure in which adults promote questioning and the enthusiastic probing of solutions.

In an optimum learning environment, teachers push kids to take risks, to try things out, to make mistakes, to learn from their errors, to experiment and create. Together, kids and adults seek to expand their knowledge and to learn how to learn. Questions are asked for both critical and creative thinking, and the answers are always too big to fully grasp. These kinds of learning places often resemble the laboratories of crazy experiments and mad thinking.

Checklist for Promoting Intelligence in a Learning Environment

How many of the following questions can you answer with an unqualified "yes"?

_____ I role model questioning.

_____ I continue to take risks to learn new things and seek new solutions.

_____ I believe learning is a process, not an event.

_____ I encourage my students to question, question, and question.

_____ I see the learning environment as a kind of laboratory where many different solutions to problems and answers to questions are tested and explored.

_____ I set up activities that engage youth of a variety of learning styles.

_____ I accept that there are many different ways of answering questions and reaching learning outcomes.

_____ I create learning challenges in which the answers are far greater than the knowledge and experience of my students and myself.

_____ I celebrate the risk taking of learners, even when they do not succeed in finding answers.

_____ I see youth as fellow explorers in the adventure of learning.

_____ I see all youth as smart.

_____ I insist that all youth see themselves as smart, even as geniuses.

Resources

The following books are recommended resources for promoting intelligence in the learning environment.

Armstrong, Thomas. *Awakening Genius in the Classroom.* Alexandria, VA: Association for Supervision and Curriculum Development, 1998.

Armstrong, Thomas. *Multiple Intelligences in the Classroom.* Alexandria, VA: Association for Supervision and Curriculum Development, 1994.

Brown, John L., and Cerylle Moffett. *The Hero's Journey: How Educators Can Transform Schools and Improve Learning.* Alexandria, VA: Association for Supervision and Curriculum Development, 1999.

Grinder, Michael. *Righting the Educational Conveyor Belt.* Portland, OR: Metamorphous Press, 1991.

5   Heart

In spite of everything I still believe that people are really good at heart.
— ANNE FRANK

Heart. Passion. Integrity. Character. Love. Courage. Persistence. I have a friend named Bill. I met him when I was teaching seventh grade social studies in a "school of last resort." He had torn up the "time out" room at his former school and was asked to leave. His reputation preceded him. Bill was a known playground fighter, disrespecter of teachers, and an all-around bad boy. About the only good thing I had heard about him was that although he was sometimes a bully, sometimes he was a defender of victims. I anticipated meeting this wild and woolly "Tasmanian devil" with some trepidation.

Bill was not easy. He terrorized his Spanish and English classes, slept through math, and excelled in sports, art, and music. For reasons I do not understand, Bill felt safe and "at home" with me. We built a close friendship and he allowed me to mentor him — although he didn't always do as I suggested. In fact, the only time his behavior improved was when he figured out for himself (with a little guidance) how to solve one of his many problems.

One day Bill left his binder and folders in my classroom. As I looked through his notes, I saw no name, no notes, and no homework files, which didn't surprise me. What did surprise me were the beautifully handwritten inspirational sayings that decorated every cover of every notebook and folder. There were the usual assortment of song lyrics — Sting, Dylan, Bono — as well as quotations from Gandhi, Martin Luther King Jr., Bobby Kennedy, and a number of writers of whom I wasn't aware but whose words were enlightening and uplifting. In addition, I found a volume of poems and lyrics for songs that he had written himself. His grade card was a mess — barely passing — but obviously, Bill's head was full of dreams, hopes, plans, and aspirations.

In his senior year, he was arrested on a school choir trip for loitering in a shopping mall. When asked to leave, he turned to the cop and made an obscene gesture. Bill was assigned a number of hours of community service

It's time we believe...

...that as educators we can make a difference in the lives of all students.

...that it takes more than money to provide children with caring, nurturing and productive educational environments.

...that students don't drop out; the system forces them out.

...that we are the most consistent and influential people in the lives of most of our students.

...that students are the potential, not the problem.

...that children need heroes and role models, and we are them.

...that every child has something to teach us.

...that medication is not the cure-all for difficult students.

...that we influence the future every time we stand in front of a classroom.

...that the littlest thing we do may make a difference in the life of a child.

...that schools being ready for all students is more important than students being ready for school.

...that every student — short, tall, skinny, heavy, clean-cut, and, yes, even those with long hair and tattoos — can grow up to be special and admirable.

From Russell J. Quaglia and Kristine M. Fox, *Believing in Achieving* (Toronto: SARS Publications, 2000), p. 134. Reprinted with permission.

and I sensed his arrest scared him. After four failing years in high school, he reached down to the passions that were always burning within him, as reflected in the quotations he had kept, and made a decision. Bill earned all A's the second semester of his senior year. At an all-school assembly, he stood in front of the junior class at an assembly and told his story. On graduation night the principal gave him a special award for having the heart and courage to turn his life around. Today Bill is married and pursuing a career in music and computer graphics.

Not every high-risk student I have worked with has secretly kept a record of inspiring words and written a volume of verse, as Bill had. But I have found that many of the toughest kids are idealists, souls filled with dreams, creative thinkers waiting to be inspired. As a teacher, I feel it is my job to not only inspire these students but also to encourage them to fulfill their aspirations with real action.

TRY THIS FOR A MOMENT:

Fold your hands interlacing the fingers and keep them there for awhile. Feels nicely comfortable, doesn't it? In fact, many people rest their hands this way.

Look at your thumbs. You will have either your right thumb over your left or your left thumb over your right.

Checklist for Promoting Heart in a Learning Environment

How many of the following questions can you answer with an unqualified "yes"?

_____ I teach and work with youth with great energy and enthusiasm.

_____ I role model the kind of character, humor, and citizenship I want to see in young people.

_____ I see achievement as more than academic success, including effort, energy, creativity, integrity, and citizenship.

_____ I establish a warm and welcoming atmosphere.

_____ I hate being bored and understand how it is for youth to be bored.

_____ I love school or my program and can't wait to get there each day.

_____ I encourage youth to demonstrate heart, effort, and integrity in their work and behavior.

_____ I create challenges for kids that are opportunities for effort, perseverance, and integrity.

_____ I establish a warm and welcoming atmosphere.

_____ I have and I encourage a real passion for learning new things.

_____ Youth love to come to my class or program and hate to leave.

_____ Youth treat me and each other with respect, and demonstrate character and integrity in their behavior.

_____ We celebrate effort, energy, positive attitude, integrity, and heart as valid achievements.

In your world that is the correct way to fold your hands — the way everyone should.

Now, re-lace your fingers so that the other thumb is now on top.

Feels awkward, clumsy, unnatural, and just wrong — doesn't it? This is how youth who are out of culture feel. Out of culture because they have a different learning style, because they have their genius on the brain's right side. Out of culture because they have different opinions, because they don't fit in, don't perform the way we do or want, because they have lost heart.

Our children lose heart only when we lose heart.

When I hear that teachers are burnt out, I wonder — as does Russell Quaglia, director of the National Center for Student Aspirations — when were they ever lit up? Whenever I work with those who work with kids, I ask them to find that place of passion, courage, and heart that first brought them to the work they do. Working with youth is difficult and involves an immense amount of energy and responsibility. But these are our children — whether we gave them life or they have wandered into ours. Our job is to light up kids, maintain the head and heart connection, inspire their dreams and personal visions, and encourage change and positive action. To do this, we must demonstrate our love for them, our passion for our work, and our own courage in everything we do with them.

School and other learning experiences must be about more than academic achievement. Character, perseverance, enthusiasm, joy, effort, and good citizenship are as important for success in life. "It's time we believe…" (see box on page 34) is a wonderful list of beliefs for teachers written by Russell Quaglia and Kristine Fox. It's time we believe that wonderful surprises are just waiting to happen, that all our hopes and dreams for our children are within reach — if only we believe.

Resources

The following books are useful resources for bringing heart into the learning environment.

Benson, Peter L., and Carl D. Glickman. *All Kids Are Our Kids: What Communities Must Do to Raise Caring and Responsible Children and Adolescents*. San Francisco: Jossey-Bass, 1997.

Benson, Peter L., Judy Galbraith, and Pamela Espeland. *What Kids Need to Succeed: Proven, Practical Ways to Raise Good Kids*. Minneapolis, MN: Free Spirit Publishing, 1998.

Lewis, Barbara A. *What Do You Stand For?: A Kid's Guide to Building Character*. Minneapolis, MN: Free Spirit Publishing, 1998.

Quaglia, Russell J., and Kristine M. Fox. *Believing in Achieving*. Orono, ME: National Center for Student Aspirations, 1998.

PART TWO

The Personal Journey

Be a lamp unto yourself. Be your own confidence. Hold to the truth within yourself, as to the only truth.

— BUDDHA

The journey to discover the wonder in life begins by opening the heart and traveling within to discover the self. In Part Two, activities are included that focus on an exploration of self:

Who am I?

What do I believe? What do I value?

What are my most central principles?

What are my dreams, hopes, and desires?

What is my mission?

The Personal Journey activities provide the basis of principle for the Reviving the Wonder group experience. As Stephen R. Covey suggests in *The 7 Habits of Highly Effective People,* how we operate in the world outside ourselves is determined by how we privately define ourselves and our principles. The creative tension of reviving the wonder in kids comes from encouraging them to reflect privately upon the experiences of their day-to-day lives while using the structured activities in this part for personal self-discovery.

The Personal Journey has the following set of outcomes for youth:

1. To develop a set of skills, tools, and practices that can be used for self-reflection and personal growth

2. To examine personal identity, principles, values, beliefs, strengths, and weakness

3. To identify personal heroes, role models, and mentors

4. To create a personal mission

5. To examine personal roles and develop specific personal action plans

6 Basic Tools and Practices

To honor, to bless, to welcome with the heart is never done in grand or monumental ways but in this moment, in the most immediate and intimate way.

— JACK KORNFIELD

The activities in this chapter are designed for use by those who will be working with a specific group of youth over a continuous period of time — perhaps in a classroom setting, during a retreat of several days, or with an on-going youth group. When constructing experiences that will take a minimum of three days (or that are extended over a semester of class time), the facilitator should repeatedly integrate three specific activities:

- Writing and/or drawing in homemade sketchbooks
- Silent reflection or meditation
- Meeting with peers for group reflection

Homemade Books

Purpose

When youth make personal books to use as journals, sketchbooks, and collections of written reflections (poetry, essays, observations), they tend to view what they write with greater value and intensity. Personal books can be used throughout a Reviving the Wonder teaching unit or retreat as a record of the experience.

Materials

cardboard

cloth

Elmer's white school glue

tape

brass tabs (three per person)

colored construction paper or a heavy-weight bond (for the inside covers)

paper cutter that will cut cardboard

color markers

pencils

scissors

hand-held hole punch

8.5×11-inch copy paper in a variety of colors

Preparation

1. Create a center for materials and tools.

2. Arrange room so participants can work at tables.

3. Punch enough of the copy paper so that each student can make a book of 100 pages.

4. Play soft music — Mozart, George Winston, or similar selections work well.

Activity Instructions

1. Out of cardboard, have the people cut two hinges and two covers as shown. The covers should be slightly larger than the paper used. If the book will use 8.5×11-inch paper, the cover should be approximately 9×11.5 inches.

2. Some creative youth might want to make a book sized to their personal taste. In that case they will need to cut paper to the size they want, make two or three uniform holes using the hand punch, and make covers slightly larger than the inside pages.

3. Have them tape hinges to covers as shown below.

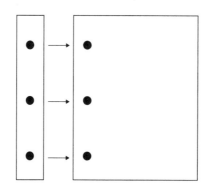 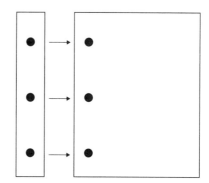

4. Cover hinges and covers with cloth. Decorate cover.

5. Glue blank paper to cover ends of cloth inside each cover.

6. Fill book with blank paper.

7. Insert brass tabs into hinges as shown to the right.

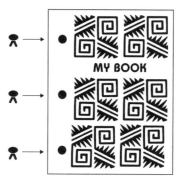

Discuss

1. What do you like about your book?

2. What do you like about the books others have made?

3. Will the book be useful?

4. What kinds of observations will you most likely include in your hand-made journal?

5. When is a good time for you to write and to sketch?

6. Where is a good place for you to write and to sketch?

7. When do ideas usually come for you? When you first wake up? When you are going to sleep? Throughout the day?

8. What is important to include when describing an activity or an experience? What kinds of details will you want to remember?

9. What kinds of things might you reflect on after an activity? What did you learn? Who did you work with? What were the insights of the group?

10. What kinds of art materials will you want to make sketches — pens, thin markers, pencils?

11. Would keeping a collection of inspiring quotations be helpful? Where would you seek these words?

12. Would you also include ideas that just come to you? Plans for your future? Dreams you dream at night? Daydreams?

Relaxation, Meditation, Contemplation

Purpose

Nearly all spiritual traditions have at their base meditation and contemplative practices. In recent years many of these techniques have also been recommended as a basis for good health. Deep breathing as a daily practice promotes greater creativity and richer thinking. Simple meditation techniques are not connected to any religious practice. They are easy to teach, hard to maintain.

Materials

Homemade books (see page 40)

Preparation

1. Schedule a time for daily relaxation.

2. Establish reflection groups, maintaining the same group membership for a number of sessions.

3. Schedule reflection group meetings on a regular basis.

Activity Instructions

During the silent period, you have a variety of choices; the common experience is silence. Possible uses for silent time are formal meditation techniques such as counting breaths or observing the mind, quiet prayer, reading, or simple quiet thought. In addition, the following activities can be encouraged:

Sketching

Sketching can be pictures or words, or both. Sketching helps intensify and preserve experiences in the moment. Encourage simple sketching, asking youth to note or draw the essentials for later reflection and more in-depth work.

Journaling

Here is a simple plan for keeping an ongoing journal. Entries should be made several times each week:

Observation: Write a detailed description of an event. Be as clear and vivid as possible in recording the event, conversation, inspiration, idea, or dream. Be as objective as possible; put off reflections and interpretations until later.

Feelings: Describe in detail any feelings evoked.

Reflections: Think about, ruminate, and process the event and your feeling reaction. Generalize and analyze. Record any ideas or further inspirations evoked.

Noting

Since inspiration comes at the oddest moments (for example, when waking from a deep sleep or in the shower), it's important to quickly jot down ideas before they evaporate.

Composing

The sketchbook is an excellent place to work on poems, essays, aphorisms, and observations. Here is the place to write and rewrite, polish and hone.

Favorite Quotes

Keep favorite lines, poems, inspirational sayings, and moving aphorisms as inspiration and support.

Planning

Create the plans for long-term projects. Sketch out ideas, try things out, and use a variety of approaches. Write out a timeline or schedule of the steps for meeting your goal.

Discuss

1. Do you notice any special themes that seem to recur in your observations and sketches?

2. What kinds of things do you tend to keep in your journal?

3. What similarities and differences do you find in your journal compared to those of others?

4. What else might you want to include?

5. Would it be a good idea to concentrate on one or two types of entries for a time?

Reflection Group Discussion

Preparation

1. Arrange a circle of chairs. It is not a good idea in a reflection group to sit around a table as this changes the tenor of the discussion.

2. You might want to select an object as a "talking stick." A talking stick was used in primitive groups to indicate who had the power to speak. In your groups, to indicate whose turn it is to speak use a small, easily handled object that has meaning for the group. Whoever holds the object has the right to speak and to decide who speaks next.

3. Ask participants to bring their journal or the object they have made in an activity to use as a source for discussion.

Materials

no materials necessary

Purpose

Through ongoing reflection discussions after periods of silence, ask questions that lead youth to share their discoveries about themselves. Most often you will find the following:

1. *Similarities are discovered.*
   There are unexpected commonalities among all people.

2. *Differences are honored.*
   Each person has unique qualities that should be cherished.

3. *Insights blossom.*
   When people open up and talk about their experiences, they learn new things about themselves. From the reactions of others, they see themselves, others, and their experiences in new and different ways.

A reflection group is primarily a discussion group. Participants are encouraged to read pieces from the homemade book and talk about recent insights. In the beginning, a number of formal activities can also be used.

The activities in Chapter 7, The Inner Me, can be used to promote reflective discussions. When you use activities where an object is made (for example, Paper People), use one session to create the object and another to engage in the reflective discussion.

Activity Instructions

1. Set the tone by discussing the purpose of the group — reminding the group of any themes they might be focusing on, summarizing the previous group if that is helpful, and announcing in general the focus of this group session.

2. Remind the group of any ground rules the group has established. Common ground rules for groups include:
   - Respect each person's opinions
   - Everything said in the group remains confidential
   - Only one person may speak at a time
   - Use the talking stick or object to indicate who speaks
   - No put-downs
   - Everyone has an opportunity to speak
   - Everyone has a right to pass

3. Ask open questions to create a free flow of discussion and reflection. Examples: "Has anyone else had a similar experience?" "How did other people handle that sort of experience?" "How many here have had that experience?" "Who would like to comment on this topic" "If this happened to you, what might you do?"

4. Paraphrase and summarize the comments of the group to seek clarity. Ask the group "Is that what you meant?" "Is that a fair summary of what has been said?"

5. Share personal experience and insights with the youth, but the focus must remain on the experiences and insights of the youth in the group.

6. Close the group. A simple closure might be some final questions, as presented in the next section.

Discuss

Monitor the group to see that everyone has an opportunity to speak.

1. Did anyone notice any common themes that came up in this discussion?

2. What did you learn, in general, about each other?

3. Did everyone have a chance to speak?

4. Did you have to take a risk to speak? Did you take that risk? What did you find out from taking that risk?

5. Did anyone want to speak but was reluctant? Why?

6. What will you take from here? What insights?

7. Did you learn anything you could use in your daily life? If so what? Where and when could you use these insights?

7   The Inner Me

I would like to beg you to have patience with everything unresolved in your heart and try to love the questions themselves as if they were locked rooms or books written in a very foreign language.... Live the questions now. Perhaps, then, someday far in the future, you will gradually, without even noticing it, live your way into an answer.

— RAINER MARIA RILKE

This chapter presents a set of activities designed to help youth examine their interiors — their inner landscapes of hopes and doubts, fears and victories, core beliefs and fleeting fantasies — thereby defining their dreams and fundamental talents. The self is always the beginning of a transformative journey. Before connecting with others, participants need to understand themselves — who they are, what they believe, and their ability to act.

Many of the activities in this chapter use personally created objects — large paper cutouts of a person's own form, a personal brochure, clay sculptures — as vehicles for looking at ourselves. When doing these activities within a school schedule, devote one period to the making of the object and another to holding small reflective discussions of the objects made. When working in a workshop or retreat venue, the making of the object flows right into small group discussion and on to the next activity.

Create a series of activities from the selection here, moving from low-risk to higher-risk activities. Sweet Talk is the lowest risk; a small group is asked to take a handful of candies and state one fact about themselves per candy piece. Because Cross the Line and Feelings Banners are whole-group activities, rather than ones in which an individual discloses personal information to others in a smaller group, these two activities provide greater safety for individuals who are skittish about disclosing personal information to larger groups. The most risky are Life Journey Map and The Mask I Wear. Both of these ask youth to look inside themselves and talk about difficult events and feelings.

Sweet Talk

Purpose

Youth have the opportunity to examine their personal characteristics and express them in a group setting.

Asset Built

#33 Interpersonal Competence

Materials

one-pound bag of candy (one per group of eight to ten youth); M&M's, Reese's Pieces, and Skittles work well

Preparation

1. Pour the candy into a large mixing bowl.

2. Arrange the group in a circle, either on chairs or sitting on the floor.

Activity Instructions

1. Pass the bowl of candy around the group circle.

2. Say to the group, "Take as many pieces as you like, but do not eat any candy until I give you permission."

3. Say to the group, "Think of all the wonderful characteristics you have as a person. Think of the many facts about your life that define you as a person. For each piece of candy you took, disclose one characteristic or fact so the group will come to know you better. You can eat a piece as you give a fact or you can wait until you have finished." Sample disclosures:

> I am 5 feet 8 inches tall.
> I am sixteen years old.
> I have a sister and a brother.
> I love to go skateboarding.
> I had a girlfriend until last week.
> My favorite movie is [movie title].
> We travel to Florida every spring break.
> I am good at soccer.
> I keep a journal.

Discuss

1. What is the most intriguing fact you heard about someone?

2. What characteristics did you disclose that were similar to several others in the group?

3. What characteristics mark each person as unique?

4. Which facts were funny? Telling? Highly descriptive?

5. If you had it to do over, would you take as many pieces of candy?

Paper People

Purpose

Youth interact while outlining each other on butcher paper. They take time for self-reflection as they decorate "themselves."

Assets Built

#37 Personal Power
#38 Self-Esteem

Materials

butcher paper
color markers
scissors
masking tape

Preparation

1. You will need to do this activity in a large room without furniture.

2. Out of butcher paper, cut one seven-foot-long banner per participant.

3. For small groups (up to twenty participants), one to three rolls of masking tape are sufficient. For groups larger than twenty, five to ten rolls will save you time and avoid confusion.

Activity Instructions

1. Create random pairs of participants.

2. Hand out two banners and one box of color markers to each pair.

3. One youth outlines the other as each lies on the butcher paper.

4. Challenge youth to decorate their "selves" in interesting and intriguing ways. Suggest using favorite quotes, personal values and beliefs, personal strengths and weaknesses, personal qualities, favorite poems, favorite phrases.

5. Hang up the finished "paper people" around the space.

6. Ask the group to do a "gallery walk," walking in silence around the room, examining without discussing each of the "paper people."

Discuss

1. Does your paper person reflect the real inner you?

2. What kinds of characters do people invent to project out to others? Do they change characters in different situations?

3. Is it scary for other people to know who you really are?

4. What positive characteristics do you like about yourself?

5. What about you would you change? How could you make this change?

Variation

1. Make a quilt out of the completed "paper people." Consider each individual sheet a piece of a quilt. Using masking tape, assemble all the pieces into a large quilt on a blank wall. Suggest to the youth that quilts often represent families or communities.

2. For discussion: How does this paper quilt represent us as a group?

Personal Mandala

LOW RISK

Purpose

Youth examine the physical, mental, social, and spiritual aspects of their lives.

Assets Built

#37 Personal Power
#38 Self-Esteem

Materials

large sheets of newsprint
color markers
Polaroid camera and film
magazines

Preparation

1. Cut large paper circles (diameters of two to three feet) out of the newsprint, one per participant.

2. Ask students to bring in a photograph of themselves and a variety of magazines they can cut up.

3. Create a model of your own to demonstrate.

Activity Instructions

1. Discuss the concept of the mandala (a circular symbol that represents the personality in various aspects).

2. Pass out the newsprint circles, one per participant.

3. Ask each person to attach a picture of him/herself at the center of the mandala.

4. Ask that each person divide their mandala into four equal sections, and label them "physical," "mental," "social," and "spiritual."

5. In each section, they should attach appropriate photographs or illustrations from the magazines and/or their own illustrations and symbols. They should also write words and phrases that represent each of the four aspects of their lives.

Discuss

1. Does one aspect of your personality dominate the others? If so, how might you go about becoming more balanced?

2. Do you feel you need to increase your involvement in any area to become more balanced?

3. What similarities and differences do you find between yourself and the others in the group? Any surprises?

Timelines

Purpose

Youth see themselves in the context of events in the world and in their communities.

Asset Built

#37 Personal Power

Materials

butcher paper
color markers
masking tape

Preparation

1. Cut three long banners of butcher paper (fifteen to twenty feet long), and hang them above one another on a wall.

2. Label the top banner "World," the middle banner "Community" (or the name of your community), and the bottom banner "Us."

3. Mark off equal sections to represent the past twenty-five years, for example:

   1975   1980   1985   1990   1995   2000

Activity Instructions

1. Ask youth to write the major historical events of the past twenty-five years on the World banner. Examples:
   Ronald Reagan elected President
   Persian Gulf War
   William Clinton elected President

2. Ask them to list the major local events of the past twenty-five years on the Community banner.
   The new high school built
   A major new industry moves to town

3. On the Us banner, personal events in their lives should be listed.
   Mom and Dad divorced
   Baby brother Jack born
   I enter first grade

Discuss

1. How are you affected by the events in your world?

2. How are you affected by the events in your community?

3. What trends do you see in the world? Which are good? Not good?

4. What trends do you see in the community? Which are good? Not good?

5. What might you do to make a difference?

Back to Back

MEDIUM RISK

Purpose

Youth learn to express feelings.

Asset Built

#33 Interpersonal Competence

Materials

list of situations that evoke
a variety of feelings

Preparation

1. This activity works best in a room without furniture where there is space for pairs of youth to sit back to back.

2. Consider allowing participants to sit on mats or pillows.

3. Create a list of situations that evoke a variety of feelings.

Activity Instructions

1. Ask participants to find a partner of the opposite sex.

2. Ask pairs to sit on the floor back to back.

3. Tell pairs you are going to suggest a number of situations that evoke feelings.

4. Suggest that humans tend to have five basic feelings: mad, sad, glad, fear, and guilt. Suggest these five feelings as appropriate responses to the situations you will be giving them.

5. Ask pairs to express to each other the feeling evoked using only their backs — no talking. (Youths will express themselves by rubbing each other's back with their own back according to their feeling.)

6. Call out each feeling-evoking situation (see examples below) and allow participants a minute or two to express their feelings, using only their backs.

> A teacher announces the duplicating machine broke and she has to postpone the big test.
>
> You thought the big test was tomorrow when, in fact, it is being given today.
>
> Your boyfriend/girlfriend sends you flowers.
>
> You hear a rumor your boyfriend (girlfriend) was holding hands with someone else.
>
> You wait all night for a call that does not come.
>
> You get picked for the team.
>
> A friend tells you she missed a period.
>
> Someone you don't hang out with makes fun of your friend.
>
> You overhear someone putting you down.

Your best friend is invited on a date by someone you were hoping would ask you.

You find the homework you thought you lost stuck in your text book.

You get an A on a test.

You are accused of something you did not do.

You made a decision and now you wish you hadn't.

Someone put you down because of your body size or shape.

You put someone down because you think they said something dumb.

You discover $20 in your wallet.

Discuss

1. How often do your feelings change during a day? An afternoon? An hour? Half an hour? A fifteen-minute period? A five-minute period?

2. Did anyone respond to a specific situation differently than your partner?

3. Did any situation not evoke a feeling?

4. What kinds of situations mostly evoked anger? Happy feelings? Sad feelings? Fear? Guilt?

5. How do you usually express each of these feelings: mad, sad, glad, fear, guilt?

6. Which feelings would you prefer to share with others? Keep to yourself? Not feel at all?

What Do I Stand For?

Purpose

Youth identify personal values and principles.

Asset Built

#28 Integrity

Materials

8.5×11-inch paper
thin color markers

Preparation

1. Use a variety of colored papers.
2. Each youth will need a colored sheet of paper. Each pair of students will need a box of color markers.
3. Create a demonstration sheet using your own foot.

Activity Instructions

1. Designate partners.
2. One partner traces the footprint of the other.
3. Ask youth to divide their "foot" into a variety of sections — up to six works best.
4. Discuss the meaning of principles, values, and beliefs.

Principles	The basic concepts, ideas, and qualities on which a person can base his/her life. Examples: honesty, integrity, humility
Values	The things a person values and wants in his/her life. Examples: friends, security, wealth
Beliefs	A person's positive beliefs. Examples: People are basically good. We should treat each other fairly.

5. Ask each person to write a word or draw a picture that reflects his/her principles. And one that reflects his/her values. Then one that reflects his/her beliefs. Allow for thinking and drawing time.
6. Combine two or three pairs of youth into small groups. Ask each person to pick a symbol to discuss. Have them use the discussion questions below.

Discuss

1. What characteristics, values, and beliefs make you unique?
2. In what ways are you similar to other people in the group?
3. What single word or symbol describes you the best?

Variation

1. Create a ten-foot-long paper banner for each small group of ten or twelve people. Have each youth in the group draw his/her foot on the banner rather than on separate pieces of paper. Then they decorate their feet as above, and tape the banner to the wall. (You'll need masking tape.)
2. For discussion: What special characteristics, values, abilities, and beliefs do you bring to this group?

Grab Bag

MEDIUM RISK

Purpose

Youth discover the positive characteristics they bring to a group.

Assets Built

#37 Personal Power
#38 Self-Esteem

Materials

brown paper lunchbags (one per person)
2×8.5-inch slips of paper (ten per person)
pens or pencils (one per person)

Preparation

1. Cut ten slips of paper per person. Scrap paper is great to use as long as one side is blank.

2. Ask youth to bring in a small brown bag or provide one small bag per person.

3. According to the instructions to the right, create a grab bag of your own to use as a model, writing ten positive characteristics you bring to a group on ten slips of paper.

Activity Instructions

1. Sit in front of the group and pull a slip of paper out of your grab bag. Read what you have written on the paper: a positive characteristic concerning what you bring to a group.

2. Pull out and read your other nine slips of paper. Give specific details and examples that show you possess each skill, talent, attitude, or characteristic.

3. Hand out bags, paper slips, and pencils or pens.

4. Ask the group: "Have any of you ever gotten a grab bag — a bag with a surprise present inside? What did you get? Were you pleased? If you were to make up grab bags for kids, what would you put inside?"

5. Say to the group: "Each of you brings to this group a unique set of attitudes, skills, talents, and characteristics that enrich this group. Think of some traits and abilities that might surprise us." Examples:

   I can juggle and if you saw me you might be entertained — and I could teach some of you how to do it.

   I take really good notes and you can read my handwriting.

6. Say to the group: "Write one trait, talent, skill, or characteristic you bring to this group on each sheet of paper. Put the slips of paper in your bag."

7. Go around the group and ask each person to reach into his/her grab bag, pull out one slip, and read it to the group.

8. Continue to go around the group until all have read their ten slips.

Discuss

1. How are we like a grab bag?

2. Were you surprised by any of the characteristics anyone talked about?

3. Where do our traits, talents, skills, and characteristics come from? Do we have a choice?

4. How many of us in this group have similar traits? Different traits?

5. Why is it good for a group of people to have a wide variety of talents and gifts?

Feelings Banners

Purpose

Youth identify and examine events that evoke inner feelings.

Asset Built

#33 Interpersonal Competence

Materials

butcher paper
color markers
masking tape

Preparation

1. Cut one ten-foot-long paper banner for each group of ten to twelve participants.

2. Each group will need one or two boxes of color markers.

3. This activity works best in a large space without furniture.

Activity Instructions

Part 1

1. Arrange participants in groups of eight to twelve.

2. Write (in large letters) one of the following words on each banner: mad, sad, glad, afraid, ashamed, confused, happy, lonely, overwhelmed, worried. If you have more than ten banners, use additional words that portray typical feelings of the age group of youth.

3. Ask each group to visit each banner and to decorate each with words, pictures, and phrases of events and experiences that evoke that feeling.

4. Groups should work at banners about five minutes.

5. Arrange banners so the groups can move, clockwise or counterclockwise, from banner to banner. Use a bell or chime to signal "time to move."

6. Ask each group to explain why they chose to put what they did on the banner.

7. When all groups are finished, tape up the banners on the walls around the room.

Part 2

1. Ask participants to move to the center of the room.

2. Ask them to walk to the banner that evokes a feeling when you either read a statement or tell a story.

   Sample statements
   How you feel about your parents
   How you feel about school
   How you feel about your friends
   How you feel about the opposite sex
   How you feel about yourself

Sample stories

A friend tells you he is afraid to go home because his dad drinks too
    much and gets violent.

A friend tells you she is having sex and is uncomfortable about it.

A friend shows you a black eye or bruise and tells you who hurt him.

A friend tells you she has discovered her dad is gay.

A friend tells you he is afraid he might be gay.

You see someone being left out because of her looks.

Discuss

1. Why did you walk to this specific banner?

2. Have you had a similar experience? What did you do?

3. What should someone in this situation do?

4. Would you react differently if the person were your best friend rather
   than a mere acquaintance?

Variations

Problem Solving Skits

1. Ask each group to examine the drawings and words on each banner.

2. Ask each group to create a skit that has the feeling word as a theme. The
   skit should first present a scene depicting a specific problem and then a
   second scene depicting a solution to the problem.
   Example
   Scene 1: an argument between parents and youth concerning curfew
   Scene 2: parents and youth discuss a reasonable time for youth to be
   home

Gallery Walks

1. Ask participants to walk in silence and examine the banners.

2. Form small groups and discuss the most compelling concerns youth have
   that were depicted on the banners.

When Am I in My Power?

Purpose

Youth identify when they feel strong, in the flow, centered, powerful.

Asset Built

#37 Personal Power

Materials

large sheets of drawing paper
color markers, crayons, or colored chalk

Preparation

1. Large sheets of newsprint work well for this activity.

2. You can use a variety of drawing materials.

3. Many stories of people experiencing their "power" can be used as examples. An especially good source is *My Spirit Flies: Portraits and Prose of Women in Their Power* by M. Cathy Angell (Bay City Press, 1997).

4. Think of several examples from your own life or the lives of people you and/or your participants might know.

5. Select soft music selections to play during the drawing — Mozart, George Winston, or similar selections.

6. Provide a space where youth can work either at tables or on the floor.

Activity Instructions

1. Introduce the concept of being "in power" — times when someone feels really good, up, powerful; when everything flows smoothly and effortlessly.

2. Explain that power here does not mean powerful over another person. Give some examples.

3. Suggest to the group that they close their eyes and relax for a moment. Ask them to let any tightness run out of their body. Then ask them to imagine a time and place when they felt really powerful. Where were they? How old? Who were they with? What was happening?

4. Ask them to slowly open their eyes and to draw a representation of when they have felt powerful in their lives.

Discuss

1. Divide people into small groups and ask each group to sit in a circle.

   Ask participants to examine each of the drawings in their group without talking or discussing.

   Ask each person to tell the others in his/her group what the picture created represents and how it makes him/her feel.

   Ask each group to figure out what "power" means. Why is it important to find and have power?

   Ask each group to choose a spokesperson.

2. With all people reassembled, ask the spokesperson from each small group to share their group's definition of "power."

When you are in your power how do you feel? How do you relate to others?

How can you use this power in the world?

Variation

When Am I Spiritual?

1. Using the same process, ask each person to remember times in their lives when they felt spiritual or connected with something greater than themselves.

2. Draw a representation of this spiritual memory.

3. Discussion questions:

What does "spiritual" mean to you?

When was the last time you felt spiritual? Who were you with? Where were you?

If you wanted to feel deeply spiritual today, where would you go? What would you do?

Personal Brochure

MEDIUM RISK

Purpose

Youth examine who they are, then identify characteristics, values, and competencies they want to develop.

Assets Built

#37 Personal Power
#38 Self-Esteem
#39 Sense of Purpose
#40 Positive View of Personal
        Future

Materials

8.5×11-inch colored paper
thin color markers
pencils
sample brochure

Preparation

1. This activity takes time and works better in a class setting than in a workshop.

2. Prior to the activity, create a sample brochure for yourself as a model.

3. Use a variety of colored papers.

4. Allow students to bring in personal photos they can cut and paste into their brochures.

5. You might want to collect a group of sample brochures; a local travel agent or office of tourism can give you a variety.

Activity Instructions

1. Discuss the characteristics of a good brochure — how it is used to promote a product or service.

2. Explain that participants are going to design a tri-fold personal brochure describing themselves.

3. On the board or flip chart, list the three areas that should be included in the brochure:

Front cover
    illustration or photograph
    graphic symbol
    name
    personal motto
    descriptive words

Inside
    personal data (for example, height, weight, health)
    assets (positive characteristics)
    values, beliefs, principles
    personal heroes, role models, mentors
    dreams and hopes for the future

Back cover
    brief biography
    family description

Variation

Using the same activity instructions, ask each person to create a second brochure that represents him/herself in ten years.

Include:

Achievements that make you proud

Contributions you have made to your family, your neighborhood, your community

Words others would use to describe you

Use the following for discussion topics:

1. What changes have occurred between the "now" brochure and the "future" brochure?

2. Examining your new brochure, what goals will you set to create this "new" you?

3. What specific steps can you take in the next several months to move toward these goals?

4. Explain that the front cover should attract readers. Ask youth to consider symbols, illustrations, and photos (or a combination) that will quickly represent their most unique qualities.

5. Give some examples of personal mottoes. Explain how a personal motto needs to reflect the values and beliefs of the individual.

6. Discuss the idea of personal assets as positive characteristics that make an indiviual unique. These might be personality characteristics, personal achievements, or accomplishments.

7. Discuss examples of values, principles, and beliefs.

8. Discuss (and list) possible heroes, role models, and mentors. You might want to create several categories:

Role Models in History (Past)

Role Models in the World (Present)

National

Regional

Local

Role Models They Know Personally

9. You might want to ask students to create a rough draft version so they can correct spelling and phrasing. Final drafts can be created on a computer (if available), or using personal printing or the best cursive handwriting.

10. Create a display area. Ask students to examine each other's brochures.

11. Ask each person to select three brochures that accurately and positively reflect the person.

12. Ask each person to find those three people and tell them why they liked these brochures.

Discuss

1. How does this brochure reflect you?

2. Are there qualities you left out? How did you decide what to include?

3. How does your motto reflect who you are?

4. What personal assets and characteristics about you do you like the most?

5. What personal assets and characteristics do you admire — in general — about others?

Keeping Each Other Afloat

MEDIUM RISK

Purpose

Youth identify actions of others that make them feel good or lifted up and those that deflate them or bring them down.

Asset Built

#33 Interpersonal Competence

Materials

large balloons
color markers

Preparation

1. This activity works best in groups of three, seated in chairs without tables.

2. Each trio will need a box of markers.

3. Each participant will need a balloon (twelve-inch balloons work well).

Activity Instructions

1. Arrange youth in groups of three, and ask them to sit knee to knee.

2. Ask each group to talk about how others' actions — what each person does or says — either inflates them or deflates them.

3. To demonstrate, ask for suggestions of how what others do inflate them. For each suggestion, blow into a balloon until it is full. Examples:
   Someone pays me a compliment
   Someone pats me on the back
   Someone helps my team succeed

4. Ask for suggestions of what it takes to make them feel deflated. For each suggestion, let some air out of the inflated balloon. Examples:
   Someone puts me down
   Someone spreads a rumor about me
   I am not invited to a party

5. Place group into triads. Ask each person to give the others positive comments or suggest ways they can inflate each other. For each positive statement, each person blows into the balloons until they are inflated.

6. Ask each person to draw a self-portrait on their balloon.

7. Ask members of each triad to write positive comments on each other's balloons.

Discuss

1. In your life who inflates you the most?

2. In your life who deflates you the most?

3. Are those who inflate and those who deflate the same people? Different people?

4. In your group or community, what can you do to inflate each other?

5. In your group or community, how can you avoid deflating each other?

Variation

Ask each triad to draw a different face on each balloon, then create a story in which the balloon faces are characters. Each group can then tell its story to the whole group.

Tri-Fold

MEDIUM RISK

Purpose

Youth examine significant events of their past and present, and look forward to their hoped-for futures.

Assets Built

#37 Personal Power
#38 Self-Esteem
#39 Sense of Purpose
#40 Positive View of Personal Future

Materials

8.5×11-inch copy paper, colors optional (one sheet per person)
thin color markers (three to five per person)

Preparation

1. Tables and chairs work well when creating the tri-folds.

2. During the discussion, have the participants sit in a circle, either in chairs or on the floor.

3. While youth make their tri-folds, play quiet music — Mozart, George Winston, or similar selections work well.

4. Create your own model tri-fold for group demonstration.

Activity Instructions

1. Use the model tri-fold you made to demonstrate.

2. Hand out one sheet of paper per person. If using colored paper, let participants select the color they want.

3. Hand out three to five color markers per person.

4. Ask students to place their papers in front of them, width-wise.

5. Ask students to fold their papers into three equal parts from right to left.

6. Ask students to open the tri-fold and write the words "Past," "Present," and "Future," one at the top of each section, on the inside of the sheet of paper.

7. Ask students to consider which events in their *past* are most significant. Use your own model tri-fold to demonstrate. Examples:

   A move from one house to another
   A divorce in the family
   Birth of a brother or sister
   A parent's new job
   Death of a grandparent
   A change of schools

8. Ask students to identify the most significant people, events, and experiences in their *present* lives. Use your model tri-fold to demonstrate. Examples:

   Parents
   Brothers and sisters
   School friends
   Personal decisions

9. Ask students to think about their deepest hopes and dreams for the *future*. Use your model tri-fold as an example. Examples:

> To go to college
>
> To get a high-paying job
>
> To get an enjoyable job
>
> To marry (or not marry)
>
> To travel

10. Ask students to decorate the outside of their tri-fold with words, pictures, and symbols that represent them as individuals.

Discuss

Form small groups of eight to twelve participants, each with an adult facilitator. Ask each person to show and talk about the information in his/her tri-fold. Use the following to discuss:

1. How do you think the events of your past affect your future?

2. What are the most significant forces in your life at present?

3. Do you fear the future? If so, why?

4. Do you look forward to the future? If so, why?

5. Thinking about the past revealed by the other members of your group, what types of events do you find you have in common? Did some of these surprise you?

6. How can you plan and prepare for your hoped-for future? What are you doing now to prepare?

Cross the Line

MEDIUM TO HIGH RISK

Purpose

Youth examine their values, beliefs, and actions, and observe those of others.

Assets Built

#28 Integrity
#29 Honesty

Preparation

You will need a large room without furniture.

Materials

no materials necessary

Activity Instructions

1. Ask youth to form two lines facing each other. Make sure there is a space of at least six feet between the lines.

2. Suggest to both groups that they are standing "on the line." Ask the members of each group to "cross the line" by stepping forward when they agree with what you say or have had the experience you describe.

3. Ask them to step back "on the line" at the end of each statement.

4. Ask the group not to discuss or make comments during the activity.

5. As you make statements or describe situations, begin with the least risky and move to more risky. For example, you could begin with: "Cross the line if you like to eat ice cream. [Pause.] And please step back." Here are some more examples:

   Cross the line if you ever…

   …worried about flunking a test

   …built a treehouse

   …lied to your parents

   …cheated on a test

   …took the blame for someone else

   …were made fun of because of how you look

   …worried your parents might get a divorce

   …lived with only one parent

   …cleaned your room without being asked

   …worried you would not be picked for a team

   …spread rumors or gossip

   …waited for a call that didn't come

   …thought others were more popular than you

   …made fun of someone else

   …worried about how you look

   …thought your family was poor

   …let someone convince you to do something you wish you hadn't

   …apologized when you were wrong

Discuss

1. Was it ever difficult to cross the line?

2. How did it feel to cross the line? With a lot of people? With a few people?

3. Did you ever not cross even when you could have?

4. Did you observe whether or not others were crossing the line? Were you surprised by who crossed (or didn't cross) the line? Do you see anyone differently now?

Variations

1. Instead of arranging the youth in two lines facing each other, arrange them in a large circle and "cross the line" into the circle. This gives the activity a different dynamic because it is easier for everyone to see each other.

2. Create statements that speak to specific themes. Examples:

Theme: *Sexual Identity*

Statement: Cross the line if you ever worried whether or not you were man [woman] enough.

Statement: Cross the line if you ever believed there are things only the opposite sex should do.

Theme: *Alcohol Abuse*

Statement: Cross the line if you ever worried about someone's drinking.

Statement: Cross the line if you've ever been to a party where someone got high.

Clay Transformations

MEDIUM TO HIGH RISK

Purpose

Youth examine the transformations in their lives.

Assets Built

#39 Sense of Purpose

#40 Positive View of Personal
      Future

Materials

play dough, modeling clay,
    or sculpting clay

paper

pens

Preparation

1. Each participant will need a supply of modeling material, a pen, and several very small pieces of paper (one inch by one inch, one for each question that you plan to ask in Part 2 of the activity).

2. Select soft music to play during the sculpting — classical music such as Mozart or soft jazz such as George Winston.

3. A room with tables works best.

Activity Instructions

Part 1

1. Create small groups.

2. Give each group a variety of colored modeling materials.

3. Explain that they are going to make a series of sculptures.

4. Ask individuals to sculpt a figure or form of where they are now in their life journey.

5. Ask them to show sculptures and discuss with small group.

6. Invite them to show and discuss with large group.

Part 2

1. Distribute small pieces of paper and pens.

2. Ask participants to put a letter, symbol, or sign that represents a larger thought or idea for each of the following phrases or statements. Suggest that they can decide for themselves which phrases or statements they wish to use:

    A hope you have for your life

    A resentment you need to let go of

    A person you need to forgive

    A forgiveness you need to extend

    A personal loss

    A sadness

    A victory or triumph

    A personal passion

    A personal dream

    A place you hope to see

    Something you hope to accomplish

3. Ask each person to push his/her tiny pieces of paper into the clay sculpture.

4. Now have them create a *new* sculpture from the same clay that represents either their present personal transformation or where they are headed in their journey.

5. Ask individuals to show sculptures and discuss in small groups.

6. Invite individuals to show and discuss with large group.

Discuss

1. What feelings were evoked with these statements?

2. What kind of support would help you on your journey?

3. What makes change difficult to handle?

4. What makes change easier to live with?

5. Is your present direction a good one?

Integrity

Purpose

Youth create a positive work ethic.

Asset Built

#28 Integrity

Materials

two flip charts
two easels
color markers

Preparation

1. Place the flip charts side by side.

2. At the top of one write: " Just Getting By." At the top of the other write: "Doing My Best."

3. Ask for volunteers who will record on each chart.

Activity Instructions

1. Ask the students their definition of the word "integrity."

2. Ask them if they know someone who has integrity.

3. Suggest to them that integrity is a quality of people who do what they say to the best of their ability. Suggest that people of integrity are authentic and congruent with themselves and with the group. People of integrity do what they say they will do and obey the rules, even when no one is watching.

4. Ask the group to think about how students "just get by" or "do their best." Example: A student who copies someone's homework while riding the bus to school is "just getting by." A student who prepares his assignments at home and does a thorough job is "doing his best."

5. Ask the group to list as many specific ways students either "just get by" or "do their best."

6. Ask the recorders to list each suggestion in large legible writing.

7. Suggest to the class that the list under "Doing My Best" is in fact a positive work ethic and an important way to work in the classroom.

8. Suggest that they might want to attempt to follow this work ethic.

9. Post both charts in the classroom.

10. Use them to point out when a student is just getting by or doing his/her best.

Discuss

1. Why is it good to do your best?

2. What happens if you just get by?

3. In your own words, explain the word "integrity."

4. Identify people who exemplify the concept of integrity.

5. What does it mean to lose integrity with yourself?

6. What does it mean to lose integrity with the group?

7. Which is more important — integrity with yourself or integrity with the group?

Life Journey Map

Purpose

Youth examine the people and events that have formed their skills, attitudes, and behaviors, and they identify hopes and dreams for the future.

Asset Built

#39 Sense of Purpose

Materials

large drawing paper
color markers

Preparation

1. Large sheets of newsprint work well for this activity.

2. During the drawing time, you might want to play soft music such as Mozart or George Winston.

3. Tables and chairs work well during the drawing portion of this activity, but discussion groups should be in circles of chairs or circles on the floor.

Activity Instructions

1. Creating your own map in front of the group, model the activity. Draw symbols of each of the below milestones as you move along a path that demonstrates your life journey:

   Where I come from
   A time I'd do over
   Some ups and downs I've had
   Where I'm heading now
   People who helped me along the way

2. Distribute drawing materials.

3. Let the group draw for about twenty minutes while you play music.

4. Place youth in small groups with an adult facilitator.

5. Let each person talk about his/her journey.

Discuss

1. Is it hard or easy for you to talk about yourself?

2. What qualities did the people who helped you have?

3. What qualities of theirs would you like to emulate?

4. What similarities and differences did you see in each other's maps?

The Mask I Wear

HIGH RISK

Purpose

Youth identify the "mask" they have created to present to others and examine their more interior personalities — the inside self they hide behind the mask. By showing others some things that are behind the mask, participants connect on a more personal level and learn some surprising things about themselves.

Asset Built

#33 Interpersonal Competence

Materials

dinner-size paper plates (one per person)
thin color markers

Preparation

1. Use paper plates — not plastic or other material — for this activity.

2. Tables and chairs work well during the drawing portion of this activity, but discussion groups should be in circles of chairs or circles on the floor.

3. Create a model of your own to use to demonstrate this activity to the group.

Activity Instructions

1. Using the model mask you have made in preparation for this activity, show the group the "outside" of your paper-plate mask, and talk about yourself and the characteristics you have that you like people to know. These can include personality traits, skills, achievements, and personal beliefs.

2. Now show the group the "inside" of your mask. Disclose those things that you are not as comfortable letting others know about you. This can include the following:

    Things you might do in secret (example: write poems only I read)

    Characteristics you might like to change (example: being late to school)

    Facts about you that few people know (example: I love to go bowling)

    Things in your life that make you angry, sad, or glad

    Hopes and dreams for the future

   As the facilitator, you must determine the level of trust in the group and how much you want to disclose. The group will go as deeply or as shallowly as the leader demonstrates.

3. Hand out the art materials.

4. Let the group draw for about twenty minutes.

5. Ask them to draw a self-portrait on the "outside" of the paper plate. (Some groups like to discuss which is the "outside" of the plate and which is the "inside.") This becomes the mask they wear in public.

6. Ask them to write (on the "outside," around the self-portrait) words that describe characteristics, traits, talents, skills, activities, hopes, and dreams they like other people to know about them.

7. Ask them to write on the inside of the paper plate words, pictures, and phrases describing traits, characteristics, facts, hopes, dreams, talents, and feelings few people know about. (See #2 in Activity Instructions, page 71.)

Discuss

Place youth in small groups with an adult facilitator. Let each person talk about the exterior and interior of his/her paper-plate mask.

1. Which was easier for you to talk about — the outside you or the inside you?

2. How did you choose what to talk about?

3. How does it feel to let people know who you are on the inside?

4. Did it surprise you to find out how others were on the inside?

5. Did you discover any similarities between you and others? Did these surprise you?

6. Will you look at others differently now?

7. What is the problem with judging people based on what they present to the world outside them?

Outside/Inside Box

HIGH RISK

Purpose

Youth examine and discuss the "outside me" (the person they want the world to see) and the "inside me" (the part they seldom let others see).

Assets Built

#37 Personal Power
#38 Self-Esteem
#39 Sense of Purpose
#40 Positive View of Personal Future

Materials

magazines
scissors
glue or paste
cardboard boxes

Preparation

1. This activity works better in classes than in workshop settings because of the time involved.

2. Each student will need a small box with a lid (a shoe box works well).

Activity Instructions

1. Discuss with youth that everybody projects a character they want others to see, while hiding who they really are inside.

2. On the outside of the box, ask the people to glue or paste pictures of what they like the world to know about them.

3. On the inside of the box, they should glue and paste pictures of who they are on the inside, the inner self they seldom show others.

4. Sit in a circle. Ask youth to talk first about their outsides.

5. Ask each student to take off the box top, and show and discuss who they are inside.

6. After each person talks about themselves, ask people to give feedback, especially if they ever thought, felt, or experienced anything similar to what any other person revealed.

Discuss

1. How different are you on the outside from the inside?

2. Are you afraid to let other people know about the inside you?

3. In what ways is your outside similar to other people on the outside?

4. In what ways is your inside similar to other people on the inside?

5. What changes would you like to make to your outside self?

6. What changes would you like to make to your inside self?

8   Heroes, Role Models, and Mentors

Without a shepherd, sheep are not a flock.

— RUSSIAN PROVERB

To develop personal character in youth, they must be asked to identify and examine the people in their lives who inspire them, who provide them support, who act as personal role models, and who take definite and specific stands based on personal values and principles. If they are to emulate these men and women, they need opportunities to look around and identify their heroes.

Many youth are inspired by the words and epigraphs of cultural heroes. They need to be encouraged to balance what they see and hear in the media with their own personal experiences, and to discern *positive* messages in the songs, films, TV shows, raps, and poetry they encounter on a daily basis.

The activities in this chapter offer youth the opportunity to consider heroism in general and then to move to more specific role models they meet in their daily lives: grandparents, teachers, other family members, coaches, and youth workers. These activities ask youth to select character traits, values, principles, and actions they see in others that they might want to emulate and integrate into their own personalities.

Heroic Quotations

LOW RISK

Purpose

Youth are inspired by the words of cultural heroes.

Asset Built

#14 Adult Role Models

Materials

books of quotations

thin color markers

8.5×11-inch paper in colors

Preparation

Gather together several books of quotations. Many are available at libraries and book stores. Two are especially good for youth and children:

Betz, Adrienne, ed. *Scholastic Treasury of Quotations for Children.* New York: Scholastic, 1998.

Sweeney, Jacqueline. *Incredible Quotations: 230 Thought-Provoking Quotes to Spark Students' Writing, Thinking, and Discussion.* New York: Scholastic, 1997.

Activity Instructions

1. Make the books of quotations available to the group.

2. Ask each person to select a number of different quotations (between three and five).

3. Ask each person to print the selected quotations on separate sheets in large letters. You might have them decorate each sheet, too.

4. Place the quotations in an area where everyone can select one.

5. Ask each person to select one that s/he finds intriguing.

6. Create smaller groups.

7. Ask each person to read his/her quotation to the group and explain why it is meaningful.

Discuss

1. Where else might you find quotations that are inspiring?

2. How do you feel when you read or hear these words?

3. In general, what are some of the common themes these quotations reflect?

4. What might you do that would put into action the themes of these quotations?

Variation

Ask students to make a collection of quotations from their favorite songs or other sources. Add these new quotations to the group collection of quotations.

Reflections on Heroic Quotations

LOW RISK

Purpose

Youth reflect on the meaning of heroic quotations.

Asset Built

#14 Adult Role Models

Materials

quotations from the Heroic Quotations activity (see page 77)
books of quotations
reflection books
thin color markers
8.5×11-inch paper in colors

Variation

1. Collect the reflections, then reproduce each one so all the students have copies of each other's work.

2. Using the directions in Homemade Books (page 40), ask each student to create a personal reflections book.

Preparation

1. This activity works best in a class setting.

2. Make available the collection of quotation books used for the Heroic Quotations activity.

3. Create a display of the quotations created in the Heroic Quotations activity.

4. Make available one or two reflection books as models. Many reflection books are available at libraries and bookstores. Hazelton and other publishers have many selections for specific audiences, including boys, girls, and young adults.

Activity Instructions

1. Ask each person to select three to five quotations from the collections or from quotations they have collected.

2. Ask each person to write a one- or two-paragraph reflection or commentary on each quotation selected.

3. Ask them to print their quotation and reflection neatly on one sheet of paper and decorate it.

4. Divide group into small groups of four or five participants. Ask each one to read his/her quotation and reflection.

Discuss

1. Did anyone discover any similarities with anyone else in the group?

2. In what ways are we different from the other members of this group?

3. Did you discover something about yourself that surprised you?

4. Did you discover something about someone else that surprised you?

5. How do you feel about the group? Are you glad you are a member? Are you comfortable with how things are going?

6. Are you comfortable with what you have disclosed to the group? Do you need any reassurance from the group?

7. Is this reflection group a meaningful experience for you? Any suggestions about changes?

Hero Collage

LOW RISK

Purpose

Youth discern the difference between positive and negative role models.

Asset Built

#14 Adult Role Models

Materials

two large paper banners

masking tape

adhesive spray

large selection of magazines
(teen, sports, news)

Preparation

1. Create a large collection of pictures of people from the magazines. If necessary, you can also make signs of famous people's names on strips of paper.

2. Cut two six-foot banners out of butcher paper and mount them on a wall.

3. Label one "Positive Role Models" and the other "Negative Role Models."

4. Cover each banner with a coat of spray adhesive.

Activity Instructions

1. Pass out the pictures and strips of paper to the participants.

2. Have each participant put the pictures on the banner they feel are appropriate.

3. If members of the group question the placement of a picture, ask the person who placed it to explain his/her reasoning.

Discuss

1. What makes each person a role model? What criteria did you use when deciding whether the role model was positive or negative?

2. Should some be moved to the opposite banner?

3. Could some be on both banners?

4. How influenced are you by celebrities? In what ways?

5. Have you ever been disappointed by a celebrity? Surprised?

Heroic Mind Web

LOW RISK

Purpose

Youth identify how heroes and role models think, feel, act, and believe.

Asset Built

#14 Adult Role Models

Materials

large sheet of paper (flip-chart size or larger)
color markers

Preparation

1. Post on a wall a large sheet of paper six feet by six feet in size.

2. Do this with a large group facing the paper.

Activity Instructions

1. Arrange the group in a half circle around a flip chart or a large sheet of paper (six feet by six feet) taped to the wall.

2. In the center of the chart, write "Heroes and Role Models." Draw a circle around these words.

3. Using a different color for each, write the following words in a different section of the chart and circle them:

   think

   feel

   act

   believe

4. Ask youth to think about heroes and role models in their lives. These are people they admire.

5. Ask them to suggest characteristics that make these people heroic. Add their suggested characteristics to the chart near the appropriate category.

Discuss

1. Can any one person possess all these characteristics?

2. Is it possible for a group to have several leaders?

3. How can a variety of leaders work in a group?

4. What characteristics of leadership do you bring to a group?

5. What characteristics do you wish you possessed?

6. What can you do to increase your leadership abilities?

Variation

If you have a large group, create smaller groups and position them around the room. Ask one person in each group to facilitate the activity. This person then follows the directions while facilitating in the smaller group.

Heroes: Think, Feel, Act

LOW RISK

Purpose

Youth examine the nature of heroes.

Asset Built

#14 Adult Role Models

Materials

flip-chart paper or newsprint
color markers

Preparation

1. This activity works well when small groups form a half circle of chairs that are facing a flip-chart stand or a piece of newsprint attached to the wall.

2. Each group will need one large piece of paper and two or three color markers.

Activity Instructions

1. Create small groups of five to twelve youth.

2. Give each group one piece of chart paper and color markers.

3. Ask each group to select a recorder.

4. Ask each group to draw a large shape of a person on the chart paper.

5. Ask each group to brainstorm and chart how they think heroes *think, feel,* and *act.* On the chart they are making, they may want to create three categories (think, feel, act) and list descriptive words under each of the three categories.

6. Ask each group to select one or two spokespersons to present their chart to the large group.

Discuss

1. What were the common findings of each group?

2. Were there any unique findings?

3. Was anything overlooked?

4. Have you ever met a hero?

5. Are there people you see every day who perform acts of heroism?

6. Can a group be heroic?

7. How could you or your group show heroism in the daily life of your school or community?

Variations

Hero Skits

1. Ask each group to create a skit that demonstrates how heroes think, feel, and act when faced with a dilemma.

2. Make sure everyone in the group has a role.

3. Ask groups to avoid easy, impossible, or unlikely solutions to the dilemma.

Hero Stories

1. Ask each group to create a story that demonstrates how heroes think, feel, and act.

2. Ask each group to select one or two storytellers.

3. Ask each group's storyteller to take notes on the story their group creates. Reassemble and have each storyteller tell the whole group the story in his/her own words.

Hero Machines

1. Ask each group to create a "human machine"; each member of the group becomes an active part of a "machine" that demonstrates a characteristic of heroism — how heroes think, feel, or act. This machine can represent a real machine; for example, a group might form themselves into the shape of a blender because leaders and heroes blend many ideas in making their decisions. This machine can also represent a made-up fantasy machine that represents a quality of heroism.

2. Make sure every person has a part to play.

3. Have each group demonstrate its machine to the entire group. See if the other groups can guess what kind of machine is presented and what heroic characteristic it represents.

4. Use the following discussion questions:

> Was this fun? What did you learn?

> How did you decide as a group what kind of machine to make?

> Who showed leadership in helping make the group decision? What kind of leadership did they show?

> Was the machine presented a good representative of the heroic quality selected?

Local Heroes

MEDIUM RISK

Purpose

Youth identify heroes in their community.

Asset Built

#14 Adult Role Models

Materials

blackboard, whiteboard, or
    flip chart

Preparation

1. Create categories to identify people in your local community who perform acts of heroism or leadership. Possible categories:

    Sports

    Community Action Groups

    Judges

    Police, Fire, Emergency Services

    Media

    Volunteers

    Government Agencies

    Politicians

    Artists, Writers

    Ordinary Citizens

2. You might want to scan the newspaper for several weeks, cutting out and filing appropriate articles.

3. For a few weeks before this activity, ask participants to keep a list of names they encounter in the news. Ask them to clip particularly compelling stories.

4. Create a series of columns on a blackboard or on flip-chart paper where you can list brainstormed names.

Activity Instructions

1. Select a person to record the names of leaders and heroes on the chart.

2. Ask the group to brainstorm. List their responses under the appropriate category of local leaders and heroes.

3. Ask each participant to select three to five names they find most intriguing or compelling, and have detailed knowledge of his/her qualifications as a leader.

4. Ask each participant to present to the group a brief discussion of the characteristics this person has as a role model, leader, or hero.

Discuss

1. What characteristics do these heroes and leaders have that you would like to possess?

2. What actions can you take now in your life to develop these characteristics?

3. What actions can you take to be more like your heroes?

4. If someone were to describe you as a leader or hero, what characteristics would they note?

Variation

Hero Interviews

1. Contact one of your local heroes and request an interview.

2. Before the interview, make a list of at least ten questions you want to ask.

3. Take a tape recorder and ask permission to tape the interview.

4. Report to the group a description of your interview experience.

5. Write and send a letter thanking the person you interviewed.

6. Discussion questions:

   Was the person you interviewed just as you imagined or different from your mental picture?

   What new information did you find?

   What characteristics about him or her do you most admire?

Animal Heroes

Purpose

Youth identify the characteristics of heroes.

Assets Built

#14 Adult Role Models
#17 Creative Activities

Materials

pictures of animals

Variation

Animal Debate

1. Have youth imagine the animals debating the most important characteristics of heroism.

2. Ask them to stage a debate, using the animal pictures to indicate which animal is speaking.

Preparation

1. This activity works best in large areas without furniture.

2. From pictures in magazines or clip art collections, select ten or twelve pictures of animals. Make sure the pictures are large enough to see across the room — 8.5×11 works fine.

3. Select several unusual animals (for example, an octopus, a zebra, or a monkey) along with animals often used to depict leadership or heroism. Lions are commonly seen as symbols of leadership, as in *The Lion King,* while eagles are seen to represent freedom of thought and the ability to see far.

4. Post the animal pictures around the room.

Activity Instructions

1. Ask the group to examine the pictures.

2. Ask individuals to cluster under the picture that most appeals to them, thereby forming small groups.

3. Ask each small group to discuss the leadership qualities the animal suggests.

4. Ask each group to select a spokesperson to report to the larger group.

5. Reassemble the group and ask the spokesperson from each small group to present the heroic characteristics of the animal they selected.

Discuss

1. Can you think of real leaders or heroes who demonstrate the characteristics represented by the various animals you've seen here?

2. If you were to select an animal to symbolize your own leadership skills, what animal would you choose?

3. If you could create a mythological beast combining the characteristics of several animals, which animals would you combine to represent heroism or leadership? (Limit yourself to no more than four animals.)

Sticky Paper Heroes

MEDIUM RISK

Purpose

Youth identify heroes and role models, and examine their lives.

Asset Built

#14 Adult Role Models

Materials

spray adhesive

butcher paper

color markers

8.5×11-inch paper (fifteen to twenty sheets)

Example

Abraham Lincoln

honest

persistent

freed slaves

saved the Union

excellent speaker

decisive

compassionate

led nation during Civil War

stayed true to his principles

Preparation

1. Cut sheets of 8.5×11-inch paper in half.

2. Create one paper wall for each group of eight to twelve participants. Each paper wall should be a rectangle of butcher paper measuring approximately ten feet by four feet.

3. Cover each paper wall with a coat of spray adhesive.

4. Divide the paper wall into three sections and label them:
   World (or Historic)   National   Local

5. Groups work best in semicircles around the paper walls.

Activity Instructions

1. Divide a large group into small groups of eight to twelve people.

2. Select a facilitator for each group.

3. Ask each participant to identify three heroes: one historic, one national, and one local or regional. Ask them to put the names of each on a separate half sheet and place them under the appropriate heading.

4. When all the heroes are placed, take down any duplicates.

5. Ask each group to select three heroes from their paper wall about whom they know a lot, one from each category. They should move the chosen names to the top of each appropriate category.

6. Ask each person to use additional half sheets to write descriptions of admirable characteristics portrayed by each hero — one per sheet. These can be attitudes, actions, beliefs, or talents. Post these under the names of each hero. At the end of this exercise, each of the selected heroes should have a list of characteristics defining them as heroes. See example to the left (Abraham Lincoln).

7. Ask each group to select three spokespersons.

8. Each spokesperson chooses one of their group's heroes and (with the help of the group) plans a short presentation. Each group will have three different presentations.

9. Ask each group to move to each wall to hear presentations. Spokespersons remain to present their topics. Ask groups to move clockwise from group wall to group wall to hear all three presentations. Give each group approximately five minutes. Signal movement by ringing a bell or chime.

Support Chart

Purpose

Youth identify adults in their lives who support them, and make closer connections with these adults.

Assets Built

#1 Family Support
#3 Other Adult Relationships
#14 Adult Role Models

Materials

blank paper, 8.5×11 inches
color markers

Activity Instructions

1. Pass out one sheet of blank paper and several color markers to each person.

2. Ask participants to draw a circle at the center of the paper and place their name inside the circle.

3. Instruct people to think about the adults in their life and — depending on how much they trust them — to write their names in different colors, close to their own name or farther away. Circle and decorate each name.

Discuss

1. Which people would you like to thank for their support? What are you willing to do to thank them?

2. Which people would you like to know better? How could you go about improving your relationship?

Variation

Set up a time for youth to plan visits, make telephone calls, and/or write letters, postcards, or email messages to those they want to thank and to those they want to get to know better.

Generation Interviews

MEDIUM RISK

Purpose

Youth discover similarities and differences concerning growing up during different generations.

Assets Built

#2   Positive Family
       Communication
#3   Other Adult Relationships
#14 Adult Role Models

Materials

note pads
tape recorders

Activity Instructions

1. Ask participants to identify people they can interview from as many generations as possible: parents, grandparents, great grandparents, uncles, aunts, older neighbors, and friends.

2. Prepare a questionnaire to use during the interviews. Recommended questions:

   What are your best memories of being an adolescent?

   What were your responsibilities?

   Who were your heroes and role models? What characteristics did they have that you admired?

   What rites and traditions did you follow in your family?

   How did you celebrate holidays?

   When and how did you come to the realization you had become an adult?

   What do you regret about leaving childhood?

   What do you like about being an adult? Dislike?

   What have been the most fulfilling events of your life?

   What do you know now that you wish you knew when you were younger?

3. Take a tape recorder with you to the interview. Ask permission to record the interview.

4. Report to the group a description of your interview experience.

5. Write and send a letter thanking the person you interviewed.

Discuss

1. What answers surprised you?

2. What similarities to your own life are there? What differences?

3. What did you learn that might help you?

Variation

Using your notes and recordings, write a short biography of the person you interviewed. Make a copy and send it with a thank-you note to the person you interviewed.

Hero Tales

MEDIUM RISK

Purpose

Youth examine the characteristics of heroes and role models in their lives. (This activity works well as a follow-up to the interview activities Local Heroes and Generation Interviews.)

Assets Built

#1   Family Support
#2   Other Adult Relationships
#14   Adult Role Models

Materials

collection of biographies, tall tales, myths, and legends (books, videotapes, and recordings)

tape recorder (if you select taped stories)

VCR and monitor (if you select video recorded stories)

8.5×11-inch three-hole paper (two or three sheets per person)

pens or pencils (one per person)

Preparation

1. Make a collection of biographies, tall tales, myths, and legends. You might want to include recordings and videotapes as well as books.

2. Select short examples of each type of hero story to read, show, or play for the group.

3. Using a hero of your own, create a story outline to tell the group a sample story. Here is an example:

> One of my heroes is my grandfather.
>
> He came to my home state at the turn of the century.
>
> He worked as a self-employed carpenter.
>
> During the depression, he and my grandmother fed three other families in our neighborhood.
>
> Although he only went through the sixth grade in school, he read the entire newspaper every day, listened to the news on the radio, and worked the crossword puzzle every night.
>
> He sent all of his children, including my mother, to college.
>
> He taught me everything I know about tools and working with wood.
>
> While he showed me how to use tools, we talked about life.
>
> I could go to him without fear whenever I had a problem.
>
> Even now when I need to figure things out, I think about what my grandfather might have said to me.

Activity Instructions

Part 1

1. Ask youth to examine the various ways stories are told about famous and heroic people. Allow them access to your collection of biographies and/or library time to do research.

2. Tell the model story. Allow others in the group to ask clarifying questions.

3. Read a selection or play a tape or show a video of example tales.

4. Ask youth to outline the story of one of their heroes or role models. They may have to do some research or interviewing to get the details.

Variations

Story Tapes

1. Allow those who do not like to speak in front of groups to tell their story on tape. (You will need one cassette per person.)

2. Make the tapes available to individuals and small groups.

3. Create a feedback sheet that listeners can fill out and give to the storyteller. The feedback sheet should ask for positive comments.

Story Books

1. Ask individuals to create at least ten drawings and ten pages of text about their hero.

2. Use the directions in Home-made Books (page 40) to create a book.

3. Arrange to have individuals read their stories to younger students.

Make sure everyone outlines a story. The outline should be a sentence outline — ten to fifteen sentences in sequence about the main points of the subject's life.

5. Encourage participants to practice telling their stories to one another.

Part 2

1. Have each person tell his/her story.

2. Set the standard that only the storyteller may speak; the others must listen in silence.

FOR ONE LARGE GROUP

Place the story circle in the middle of the room. Ask for volunteers to go first, or have each person draw a number to decide the order of the storytelling. Allow the others to gather around the storyteller.

FOR SEVERAL SMALLER GROUPS

Everyone can tell a story in the story circle. Arrange each small group in a circle, with people seated in chairs or on the floor.

3. Sit in a circle and swap tales. Youth can embellish stories if they wish.

Discuss

1. What characteristics, values, beliefs, and principles did each hero have in common?

2. What characteristics, values, beliefs, and principles would you like to have?

3. If someone told a tale about your group, what would they tell?

9   Connecting with Others

When spiderwebs unite they can tie up a lion.

— ETHIOPIAN PROVERB

The set of activities in this chapter takes a random group of individuals and moves them into relationship with each other. As a group, they are able to commit to each other and to the group as a whole. At least for the duration of the learning experience, they become a community willing to engage in the activities presented by the leader and willing to work as a group to find solutions to challenges. Within an appropriate framework of basic principles, values, and agreements, the community created by the group becomes a metaphor for real-life communities.

Moving a collection of random individuals into a group committed to a set of guiding principles and ready to take on challenges as a community takes leadership from the facilitator. (For a fuller description of this process, see Chapter 1, Hope.) A sequential series of activities should be followed that includes the following:

- Presenting a set of themes and getting agreement to guiding principles for the learning experience.

  Example: We are here today to have a great time but we are also here to examine ourselves as growing men and women and how we treat each other.

- Soliciting a set of ground rules and getting agreement from the group to follow them during the event.

  Example: For us to work effectively as a group, what rules and agreements might we want to live by today?

- Providing the group with a common set of experiences. If the sequence of activities builds from low risk to higher risk, group members will grow to know and trust one another more easily and freely.
  Example: Activities in which the entire group is working together (see Shapes, page 94) are lower risk than those activities that call for smaller groups, those that call for physical touch (see Body Part Connections, page 104), and those that involve trust (see Give Me a Lift, page 108).

- Asking open questions and leading short discussions that focus on discovering similarities within the group.
  Example: How many in this group were apprehensive about taking this risk? How many did? How many are glad they did? What did you learn?

Unless the group is guided to this We stage (as described on page 8), the specific work of the class, retreat, or workshop cannot be accomplished. It is crucial that the leader create and facilitate a sequence of community-building activities before proceeding to those that deal with the specific theme of the learning experience. The facilitator knows s/he has succeeded in guiding the group into a bonded community when individuals willingly participate in the activities, laugh freely, and refer to themselves as "we."

Circle of Life

LOW RISK

Purpose

Youth examine their relationship with the whole group.

Assets Built

#33 Interpersonal Competence

Materials

no materials necessary

Preparation

This activity works best in a large room without furniture.

Activity Instructions

1. Begin with the participants standing in the center of the room.

2. Ask youth to think of their birth dates (month and day).

3. Remind the group to remain silent until you discuss the activity.

4. Ask youth to form a single circle around the room in the order of their birth.

5. Stand in one spot to the side of the room. Say: "When you are finished making the circle, the person born closest to January 1 should be here on my right and the person born closest to December 31 should be here on my left. Everyone else should be in the order of their birth. Remember to maintain silence and find nonverbal ways to get to your place in the circle."

6. Check to see if all participants were able to find their spot, and celebrate their success.

Discuss

1. Do you choose to be born on a certain day?

2. How is the circle a symbol of equality?

3. How did you find your place in the circle?

Shapes

LOW RISK

Purpose

Individuals in the group learn to work as a community.

Asset Built

#34 Cultural Competence

Materials

no materials necessary

Preparation

This activity works best in a large room without furniture.

Activity Instructions

1. Form a birthday circle (see Circle of Life on page 93).

2. Ask the group to "think as a community" while forming, as a whole group, various shapes. Request that they move in silence, taking as few steps as possible. Sample shapes:

   The number 2
   The number 4
   The letter R
   The letter S
   Plus sign
   Multiplication sign
   Division sign
   Fractions 1/2, 1/3, 1/4
   Mouse
   Elephant
   Horse
   Whale
   Olympic rings

3. For those who seem stuck, suggest that they imagine they are up in the sky looking down at the group forming the shape.

Discuss

1. How did you work together?

2. Were there leaders?

3. How did you communicate?

4. How did you use your imagination?

5. What was difficult?

6. How is life like this?

Reach Out and Touch Someone

LOW RISK

Purpose

Youth interact and meet one another.

Assets Built

#33 Interpersonal Competence
#34 Cultural Competence

Materials

no materials necessary

Preparation

1. This activity works best in a large room without furniture.

2. Create a list of personal characteristics; see step 3 (to the right) for examples.

3. If you are working on a specific theme, try to create statements that reflect that theme.

Activity Instructions

1. Start with everybody standing in the middle of the room.

2. Ask youth to mingle throughout the room.

3. Call out a characteristic. Ask that the people find someone in the group who has that charactistic, and touch that person. (In new groups or among those who lack trust and have safety issues, ask people to "touch" by using two fingers on the shoulder.) Sample characteristics:
   Touch someone
   …who is wearing glasses
   …who is wearing red
   …you have never met
   …you would like to know better
   …who's ever felt lost, lonely, or afraid
   …who likes a kid cereal for breakfast
   …who used to wear footed pajamas
   …who has lived in another country
   …who eats a lot of pizza
   …who can run really fast
   …with the same color eyes as you
   …with the same color hair as you
   …taller than you
   …you would like to have lunch with

4. Call out another characteristic, and again ask that people find and touch someone who has that characteristic.

5. Do fifteen to twenty rounds.

Discuss

1. Was it difficult to touch other people?

2. Did you feel uncomfortable being touched?

3. Did you notice anything new about people in this group?

4. Did this activity make you more observant of others?

5. How is this activity like life?

I Got You Now!

LOW RISK

Purpose

Youth meet one another.

Asset Built

#34 Cultural Competence

Materials

I Got You Now! worksheet
(see page 97)

pencils

Preparation

Duplicate the worksheet on page 97, one per participant.

Activity Instructions

1. Distribute activity sheets and pencils.

2. Ask group to read the directions on the sheet with you.

3. Give the group approximately fifteen minutes to complete the sheet.

Discuss

1. Did you have fun?

2. Did you meet anyone you didn't know before today?

3. Did anyone surprise you?

4. Was it difficult for you to ask others to do silly things?

5. Was it difficult for you to do silly things?

I Got You Now!

Directions

Do the following ten tasks. Each task requires the involvement of at least one other person.

For each task, work with different people — no duplicates, please.

The Ten Tasks

1. Untie someone's shoe, then tie it again.

    Have the person sign here: _____

2. Count out loud (as loud as you can) as you do ten jumping jacks with a partner.

    Have your partner sign here: _____

3. Find someone who is left-handed.

    Ask him/her to make a right-handed signature here: _____

4. Ask someone to do five push-ups for you and sign here:

    _____

5. Find someone who has the same color eyes as you. Have him/her sign here:

    _____

6. Find four people, sit in a circle, and sing the alphabet song. Have these four people sign here:

    _____   _____

    _____   _____

7. Form a circle with four new people. Impersonate a cow, a horse, a pig, and a chicken. Have these four people sign here:

    _____   _____

    _____   _____

8. Find four new people. Stand in a circle and sing a TV commercial. Have these four people sign here:

    _____   _____

    _____   _____

9. Get a penny from someone. Have him/her sign here:

    _____

10. Find four other people and have a group hug. Have these four people sign here:

    _____   _____

    _____   _____

Thank You Very Much, But I Gotta Go

MEDIUM RISK

Purpose

Youth meet one another.

Assets Built

#33 Interpersonal Competence
#34 Cultural Competence

Materials

list of conversation topics

Conversation Topics

Describe your best friend in first grade and why you liked him/her.

Describe a teacher you really like.

Describe someone you respect.

Describe the weirdest food you've ever eaten.

Describe your favorite method for driving your parents crazy.

Describe the characteristics in your friends that drive you crazy.

Describe the funniest thing you can remember happening in your elementary school.

Preparation

1. This activity works best with large groups (twenty or more) in a large room without furniture.

2. Make a list of twenty conversation topics (see examples to the left).

Activity Instructions

1. Form a birthday circle. (See Circle of Life, page 93.)

2. Ask the participants to count off 1-2, 1-2.

3. Ask the 2s to step forward one step, turn around, and stand in front of the closest 1 to their right.

4. Follow this pattern:

   Ask pairs of youth to say hello, shake hands, and find out each other's name.

   Assign a conversation topic for this round.

   After a short conversation (about two or three minutes), ask them all to say "Thank you very much." (Wait for them to repeat after you.) "That was cool" (they repeat) "but I gotta go" (they repeat).

5. Then ask the group to move. For example, say "All 2s, move three people to your right." Keep moving the group until most people have met each other and had a short conversation.

6. For each round, assign a different conversation topic.

Discuss

1. Did anyone's answers surprise you?

2. Was it difficult to meet and converse with new people?

3. Did you find most people had experiences similar to yours? Different from yours?

Circles and Circles

MEDIUM RISK

Purpose

Youth meet in a series of random circles and get to know each other.

Assets Built

#33 Interpersonal Competence
#34 Cultural Competence

Materials

no materials necessary

Preparation

This activity works best in a large room without furniture.

Activity Instructions

1. Start with everyone in the middle of the room.

2. Say to the group: "I am going to ask you to sort yourselves into a series of smaller groups. Each time I raise my fingers in a number, you must create a new group with at least that many people. You must work with different people for each new grouping." Move from larger to small groups.

3. For each group formation, ask one question, moving from easy to more complicated or more risky questions. Sample questions:

    Find out from everyone in your group:

    Favorite color

    Favorite food

    Favorite holiday

    Find out who has:

    The largest family

    The longest hair

    The biggest feet

    The smallest feet

    Find out from each person in your group the funniest or most unusual thing s/he can remember from elementary school.

    Find out from everyone in your group the most unusual thing they have seen looking out of a window of their home.

    Describe for each other a teacher or coach you loved.

    Find out from each other:

    Something you hope to accomplish

    A place you'd like to visit

    A dream you hold in your heart even though it seems impossible

Discuss

1. Did you learn anything new about people you might have known for some time?

2. Were you surprised about what you learned? In what way?

3. What can you say, in general, about people you meet?

Mingle, Mingle
MEDIUM RISK

Purpose

Youth discover new things about each other.

Asset Built

#33 Interpersonal Competence

Materials

8.5×11-inch paper (one per person)
color markers (one per person)

Preparation

1. Create a sample "Ask Me About" sheet to model this activity.

2. This activity works best in a setting where participants can freely move about.

Activity Instructions

1. Pass out paper and marker to each person.

2. Ask youth to write the words "Ask Me About" at the top of the sheet of paper.

3. Ask youth to think of three things other people usually ask them, and then write (using large letters) these three topics on their sheet of paper. Examples:

    My weird pet   My favorite foods

    My brothers and sisters My trip last summer

    My favorite sport   My unusual hobby

4. Ask everybody to stand in a mix in the center of the room, each person holding his/her sign out for others to see.

5. Give a signal and ask the people to mingle. Wait about thirty seconds.

6. Give another signal for them to stop and talk to one another in groups of two or three about what's on their sign.

7. Do three to five rounds.

Discuss

1. What unusual things did you find out about other people?

2. What similarities did you discover?

3. Did you find it difficult to talk with other people? Easy?

Variation

1. After several rounds, ask the last pair to sit facing each other on the floor or in chairs.

2. Ask the partners to interview each other. Suggest a topic. Sample topics:

    Five things about the music you love

    Three things you love to do when you have nothing to do

    Your favorite ways of driving your family crazy

    Something that scares you

    Someone you admire

    Something good you hope happens to you this year

3. Ask partners to introduce each other to the reassembled group.

Frog Flipping
MEDIUM RISK

Purpose

Youth learn to work together as a team.

Assets Built

#33 Interpersonal Competence
#34 Cultural Competence

Materials

six large plastic frogs (or six bean bags or six pairs of rolled up sox) for each group of eight to ten students
bell or whistle

Preparation

1. Collect the necessary props (frogs, bean bags, or socks).
2. This works well in a large room without furniture.

Activity Instructions

1. Place youth in random groups of eight to ten students.
2. Ask each group to form a circle.
3. Place six frogs (or bean bags or socks) in the center of each circle.
4. Say to all the groups:
   "When I blow the whistle, your group is to figure out how to juggle all six frogs. Every person in the group must touch all the frogs. The frogs must go up into the air. You might want to start with one frog and make a pattern. Your team is a success when you can juggle three frogs. You are masters when you can juggle all six frogs and keep them going."
5. Allow enough time for most groups to master the challenge. Blow the whistle again to end the activity.

Discuss

1. Was your team successful?
2. How many frogs did you manage to juggle?
3. Who showed leadership?
4. Did you have to change your pattern?
5. Did you get bored?
6. What were the key elements of your success?

You Send Me

MEDIUM RISK

Purpose

Youth learn to work as teams.

Asset Built

#33 Interpersonal Competence

Materials

no materials necessary

Preparation

1. This activity works best with large groups in a large space without furniture.

2. Create a list of tasks you want the teams to perform.

Activity Instructions

1. Stand in center of room.

2. Form groups of six to twelve participants in each group.

3. Tell groups you are going to ask them to do a number of things. Tell them when all the teams have completed the task, you will go to the next task.

4. Tell teams that each round they should send you a new person to get directions.

5. Shout "Send me someone new!" and give the team representative a new task. Here are some fun tasks teams like:

> Stand in a circle, hopping on one foot while singing the "Alphabet Song."

> Stand in a circle, shortest to tallest.

> Stand in a circle, youngest to oldest.

> Stand in a circle in numeric order according to the number in your home address.

> Bring me a house key, a library card, a driver's license, a dollar bill, and a bracelet.

> Bring me something you wear on your head or in your hair, a credit card, a penny, a nickel or a dime, a piece of jewelry, a handkerchief.

> Bring me five shoelaces tied in bows end to end.

> Think of the Golden Gate Bridge, the George Washington Bridge, or any suspension bridge. Have all your teammates build a suspension bridge.

> Have all your teammates create a helicopter. Be sure to have a cockpit, top blade, and back rotor.

> Lying on the floor, ask your teammates to spell the name of your school's mascot.

Discuss

1. Did you have fun?

2. Did you find yourself competing with other teams?

3. Were you successful?

4. What are the key ingredients of your success?

5. What do teams need in general to be a success?

6. Have you ever been on a team that was a success but you didn't have fun? If so, why?

7. Have you been on a team where you had fun but didn't find success? If so, why was it fun?

8. Who showed leadership? How?

9. Why are leaders important?

10. Do you feel closer now to your teammates? Trust them more?

11. Did you work with someone you don't know well? Was that okay?

12. Do you see any of your teammates in a new way? If so, how?

Body Part Connections

MEDIUM RISK

Purpose

Youth meet one another and connect in new ways.

Asset Built

#33 Interpersonal Competence

Materials

list of appropriate body
  connections
list of conversation topics

Conversation Topics

Your greatest accomplishment so
  far in your life
Most important attribute you seek
  in a friend
Characteristics you bring to a
  friendship
Your favorite food to eat on your
  birthday
Three things to do when you
  have nothing to do

Preparation

1. You will be asking pairs of students to connect two or three body parts to each other, then to hold the pose they create while they converse for about thirty seconds.

2. Ahead of time, make a list of appropriate connections you will want to call out to the group, as well as a list of conversation topics.

3. This activity works well with large groups in a large room without furniture.

Activity Instructions

1. Stand in center of room and pair up the participants.

2. Call out two body parts and ask each pair to connect one part from one person to the second part of the other person. Examples:
     Forehead to ear
     Elbow to hand
     Hand to foot

3. When the majority of pairs have achieved the called-out connection, ask them to discuss one of the topics you prepared while holding these positions. (See sample conversation topics to the left.)

4. After approximately thirty seconds, say: "Okay, mingle, mingle." (Allow them to mingle for about one minute.) "Stop. Find a new partner and pair up. Connect these new body parts." (Give them a new set of parts to connect.)

5. Give a new conversation topic.

6. Let the group mingle, find new partners, connect, and discuss — for seven to ten rounds.

Discuss

1. Was it difficult to touch others?

2. Did anyone feel uncomfortable? Comfortable?

3. How is this activity like life?

Aces and Faces

Purpose

Youth discuss the formation and influence of cliques.

Asset Built

#5   Caring School Climate

Materials

deck of playing cards

Preparation

1. This activity works best in a large room without furniture.

2. If you have more than fifty-two people, you will need two decks of cards.

Activity Instructions

1. Start with the group in the middle of the room.

2. Shuffle the cards. Deal them out, face down, one to a person. Ask that no one look at his or her card.

3. At a signal, ask everyone to hold their card (without looking at it) on their forehead, facing out.

4. Ask everyone not to tell each other the type of card being shown.

5. Suggest to the group that they are all new students at a new school. It's the first day. Say: "You are going to wander through the room, looking for people you might like to befriend or hang out with." This is how you will decide:

   Remove the jokers.

   Aces are really terrific; they fit into all groups.

   Face cards are really cool; you really want to know them.

   Numbers 5 through 10 are neutral; you decide on the spot.

   Numbers 2 through 4 are losers; avoid them.

6. Allow the participants to mingle for awhile. Usually the larger group breaks into small groups (cliques) according to the numbers or faces on their cards. They will do this naturally. The 2s, 3s, and 4s will either stand alone or form small groups.

7. When you see the group has formed smaller groups, ask the group to freeze. Then ask them to look around and see how the group has sorted itself.

8. Ask individuals to look at their cards, then reassemble as a large group.

Discuss

1. Is school like this? Is life? How?

2. How do groups form? On what basis? Is it fair? Does it make sense?

3. Did you become part of a group or stay an individual?

4. How do you feel about the group in which you found yourself?

5. Could you tell what kind of card you were? Did you like it?

6. How do you feel about cliques?

Great Escape

Purpose

Teams work together and build alliances.

Asset Built

#34 Cultural Competence

Materials

one ball of yarn for each team of ten to twelve (enough to create a square ten feet by ten feet)

Preparation

This activity works well with large groups in a space without furniture.

Activity Instructions

1. Place youth in groups of ten or twelve.
2. Ask four members from each team to form a large square with the yarn, each youth standing at a corner of the square while holding the yarn waist height and stretching it taut.
3. Ask the remaining team members to assemble in the middle of the square.
4. Suggest to them that the yarn is the top of a fence. The fence extends to the ground. Suggest that the square is a prison. In order to escape they must help their teammates over the fence without touching it.
5. The four people holding yarn only form the square and do not escape.
6. IMPORTANT: If anyone touches the fence at any time, all team members (including those who have successfully escaped) must return to the center of the square and start over.
7. As teams finish they can watch the remaining teams.

Discuss

1. What were the elements to your success?
2. How did you work together?
3. In life, how do we help each other through difficult times?
4. What part did you play in helping your team escape? Lead? Suggest ideas? Actively support the team?
5. How is this activity like life?

Circle of Support

HIGH RISK

Purpose

Youth identify those in their lives who support them and examine how they provide support to others.

Assets Built

#1   Family Support
#14 Adult Role Models
#33 Interpersonal Competence

Materials

no materials necessary

Preparation

This activity works best in a large room without furniture.

Variation

After this activity, give each person a large sheet of paper and a pencil.

1. Ask each person to draw a circle in the middle and write his/her name inside the circle.

2. Ask each person to draw a series of circles around the central circle; in each new circle, participants should write the names of people in their life who give them support.

3. Provide color markers and other art supplies so the charts can be decorated.

4. Display the charts in the room.

Activity Instructions

1. Place youth in groups of ten or twelve.

2. Ask them to stand in a circle, shoulder to shoulder, with one volunteer in the middle.

3. The person in the middle must keep his body stiff, cross his arms over his chest, and keep his feet together. He is the person to be supported.

4. The people standing in a circle are the supporters. Each person must work with the person to the right and to the left to support the person in the middle. Ask the supporters to put one foot behind the other and keep their knees unlocked and flexible. Ask them also to put their hands up to chest or shoulder height so they can catch the person in the middle.

5. Ask everyone to repeat this pledge: "I promise to support you and keep you up. I won't let you down. You can depend on me."

6. When the person in the middle is ready to be supported, ask him/her to say, "Team ready?" When the supporters are ready, they should respond, "Ready!" Then the person in the center of the circle knows it's safe to lean back. Supporters gently move him/her about the circle. When s/he is ready to stop s/he says, "Stop," and the team stands him/her up.

7. The person who was in the middle takes a place standing in the circle, and the next person steps into the circle. When the person in the middle is ready to be supported, s/he says, "Team ready?"

8. The process is repeated until everyone gets a turn in the middle.

Discuss

1. Did you trust your team? Was it a risk?

2. Who do you trust to support you in life?

3. How do they support you?

4. Who trusts you? How do you support them?

Give Me a Lift

HIGH RISK

Purpose

Youth learn to work together, trust each other, and take care of each other.

Asset Built

#33 Interpersonal Competence
#34 Cultural Competence

Materials

no materials necessary

Preparation

1. This activity works best in a large room with no furniture.

2. Practice this activity with a small group first so they can easily demonstrate for the larger group.

Activity Instructions

1. Form groups of twelve to fifteen.

2. Call forward the demonstration group. Ask for a volunteer.

3. Tell the volunteer to make his/her body stiff. Ask the demonstration group to gather around the volunteer.

4. When the volunteer is ready, s/he says: "Team ready?"

5. When the team is ready, they say in unison: "Ready!"

6. The volunteer leans back and the team lifts the person into the air, up to eye level or slightly above.

7. The team gently moves the person around the room one time, and then gently places him/her back on the ground, feet first.

8. Instruct the groups to try this, giving every person the opportunity to be lifted.

9. Make sure all people on the team participate by lifting.

Discuss

1. How did it feel to go up?

2. Did you take a risk?

3. Did you learn you could trust your group?

4. What did you learn?

5. How is this activity like life?

Personal Attachments

HIGH RISK

Purpose

Youth honor each other as women and men.

Asset Built

#38 Self-Esteem

Materials

small slips of paper (approximately 300)

masking tape (one roll per small group)

color markers, pencils, or pens (one per person)

Preparation

1. Cut up paper until you have approximately 300 pieces about the size of a small index card (3×5 inches).

2. Arrange the room to accommodate several small groups of people sitting in chairs in the shape of a circle.

Activity Instructions

1. Create small groups — either same sex or mixed — and ask them to sit in circles.

2. Ask one person from each group to stand or sit in the center of the circle.

3. Ask the others to write positive statements about the person in the middle, one per slip.

4. Ask each person to read the slip s/he wrote and then tape it to the person in the center of the circle. (If time permits, participants can write on more than one slip for any given person.)

5. Call for a movement of people around each circle, with a new person coming into the middle and the person in the middle taking a chair. Repeat until all people have had a turn in the center of the circle.

6. Encourage everyone to write at least one comment per person.

Discuss

1. What did you like about this experience? How did you feel?

2. Were there any surprises?

3. How can you support each other on a daily basis?

4. Is there anyone in your life who would appreciate a phone call or a note, giving them positive comments?

Adapted from "Dressing Up," Michelle Karns, *How to Create Positive Relationships with Students: A Handbook of Group Activities and Teaching Strategies* (Champaign, IL: Research Press, 1994), p. 106.

Clearing a Conflict

Purpose

Youth learn a simple process for resolving a conflict.

Assets Built

#28 Integrity
#29 Honesty
#36 Peaceful Conflict Resolution

Materials

flip chart
color markers
Conflict Description worksheet
   (see page 114)
demonstration Role Play Script,
   two copies (see page 115)
pens or pencils

Launching Points

1. What are the most common kinds of conflicts you see on campus? In your community? In the world at large?

2. What are the most common kinds of conflicts among your friends?

3. How do you and your friends usually resolve conflicts?

4. Ask youth to identify the solutions that are violent.

5. Ask youth to identify the solutions that ignore the problem.

6. Ask youth to identify the solutions that satisfy both people in the conflict (i.e., solutions that are effective in resolving conflicts).

Preparation

1. This activity works well in groups of fewer than twenty.

2. Make a poster that outlines the four-phase clearing process.

   Phase One: State the Data
     Ask to be heard.
     Objectively describe what happened.

   Phase Two: State Your Feelings
     Mad? Sad? Glad? Afraid? Guilty?

   Phase Three: State Your Judgment
     What is your interpretation of what happened?

   Phase Four: State What You Want
     To resolve the conflict, what do you want from the other person?

3. Arrange the chairs in a semicircle facing the poster.

4. Set up two chairs facing each other for the demonstration.

5. Make copies of the Conflict Description worksheet, one per participant.

6. Make two copies of the demonstration Role Play Script.

Activity Instructions

Session One

1. Hold a discussion about conflict situations. Use the questions to the left as launching points.

2. Hand out one Conflict Description worksheet to each student. Ask the students to fill them out.

3. Pair off the students in twos. Ask each student to compare and contrast his/her conflict situation with his/her partner.

Discuss (Session One)

1. Did you find any similarities in the kinds of conflict situations each of you experienced? Any differences?

2. Did any of your conflict situations seem humorous when viewed objectively?

3. Did any of your conflict situations renew your feelings of anger?

4. Did you feel better after describing your conflict and talking about it?

5. What kinds of solutions did you discover? Did they resolve the conflict?

6. Are you still in conflict with the person you described on your Conflict Description worksheet?

Session Two

1. Explain to the group that you are going to teach them a simple way to resolve conflicts. Using the poster, explain each of the four phases. Here are some important points to cover in your explanation:

   Phase One: State the Data

   When a person wants to confront another, s/he must first ask to be heard. When the second person agrees to listen, the first person describes what s/he experienced as objectively and clearly as possible.

   Example: John, will you listen to me for a moment? (Wait for a "yes" before continuing.) Yesterday I asked you to call me and give me some important information. I called you to remind you and you said you were eating dinner, but you also said you would call me as soon as you were finished. I waited two hours and you didn't call. When I called you back, I got your answering machine.

   Phase Two: State Your Feelings

   Clearly state your feelings. The five most common feelings are mad, sad, glad, afraid, and guilty. In most situations of conflict, you will feel angry.

   Example: I felt really angry when you didn't call me.

   Phase Three: State Your Judgment

   It is important to clearly state your judgment or interpretation of the event.

   Example: My judgment is that you don't respect me or think calling me is very important.

   Phase Four: State What You Want

   Clearly describe what you want from the other person.

   Example: I want you to follow through when you make me a promise.

2. Ask two students to role play the script provided on page 115. As the actors present the scene, stand at the poster and point to the phase being performed.

3. Ask the students to read the script again, but this time the two students should stop when they finish one of the four phases. Point out to the group how each phase works.

4. Have the students join the partner from Session One. Ask each pair to create a scene that demonstrates the four-phase clearing process. (See suggested role play situations below.)

5. Ask each pair to perform their example. (If your group is larger than twelve, create groups of twelve in which six demonstrations will be performed.) As each pair performs their scene, ask another student to point to the phases presented using the poster.

6. After each role play, ask the student audience these questions:

Was the role play realistic?

Did the person confronting the other clearly state the data? His/her feelings? His/her judgment? A clear request?

Was the conflict resolved?

Do you have any suggestions for the actors to improve their skills?

Role Play Situations

NOTE: The best role play situations are those identified by the students. Ask them to identify common conflicts, and write their suggestions on a flip chart. Here are some other examples you might want to use:

During a phone conversation, you tell a good friend your dad was fired from his job. The next day another friend asks you if it is true.

You and a friend are working on a project for school. You check out a library book with the understanding the other person will return it. You receive an overdue notice from the library.

You hang out with a friend who lives next door in your neighborhood. At school she has another set of friends and ignores you when you come up to talk.

A friend tells you that another friend told him you were having sex with your girlfriend.

When you walked by, a classmate made a negative comment about your body shape.

Without your knowledge or involvement, a friend copied answers from you during a test. The teacher thinks you both were cheating.

Discuss (Session Two)

1. Do you think the four-phase clearing process is a good way to confront someone who has wronged you in some way?

2. What would make it difficult to use?

3. What makes this a better way of handling conflict than what you have been doing?

4. Where in your life can you use this process?

Conflict Description

1. With whom have you had a recent conflict?

2. Where were you when you had the conflict?

3. What time of day was it?

4. Is this someone you often have conflicts with?

5. What specifically happened? What was the conflict about?

6. How angry were you? Use this scale to indicate how angry you were:
   Low   1   2   3   4   5   6   7   High

7. How did you handle the conflict?

8. Is the conflict resolved?

Role Play Script

Bill: Hey, Jake, could I talk with you?

Jake: Sure.

Bill: Yesterday you invited me to come over to your house after school. I told you I had to do some errands for my mom but I would be over after I finished them. When I got over to your house, your mom told me you were at Bob's house.

That made me sad at first. Then I got angry.

This makes me think you like Bob better than me and would rather hang out with him.

I want you to respect me, and when you make an agreement with me I want you to take it seriously.

Jake: Bill, I like hanging out with you. When I got home Bob called and told me he just got a hot new electronic game. I wanted to see it. I just forgot you were coming. I messed up. Maybe we could get together tomorrow afternoon.

Asking Forgiveness

HIGH RISK

Purpose

Youth learn a simple process for asking for forgiveness.

Assets Built

#33 Interpersonal Competence
#36 Peaceful Conflict Resolution

Materials

flip chart
color markers
Forgiveness Situation worksheet
 (see page 120)
demonstration Role Play Script,
 two copies (see page 121)
pens or pencils

Discussion Launchers

1. Have you ever done something you wish you hadn't? Was your regret based on the fact that you got caught? Was your regret based on the realization that you hurt someone's feelings? Was your regret based on your feeling of guilt (because you know what you did was wrong)?

2. Have you ever wished you could make amends or ask for forgiveness?

3. Why is asking for forgiveness difficult?

4. Would there be fewer conflicts if people asked for forgiveness?

Preparation

1. This activity works well in groups of fewer than twenty.

2. Make a poster that outlines the four-phase clearing process (or use the poster you made for Clearing a Conflict on page 110):

   Phase One: State the Data
     Ask to be heard.
     Objectively describe what happened.

   Phase Two: State Your Feelings
     Mad? Sad? Glad? Afraid? Guilty?

   Phase Three: State Your Judgment
     What is your interpretation of what happened?

   Phase Four: State What You Want
     To resolve the conflict, what do you want from the other person?

3. Arrange the chairs in a semi-circle facing the poster.

4. Set up two chairs facing each other for the role plays.

5. Make copies of the Forgiveness Situation worksheet, one per participant.

6. Make two copies of the demonstration Role Play Script.

Activity Instructions

Session One

1. Hold a discussion about conflict situations. Use the questions to the left as launching points.

2. Ask students to give you some suggestions based on situations they have witnessed where one person needs to ask forgiveness from another. List these on a flip chart.

3. Hand out one Forgiveness Situation worksheet to each student. Ask the students to fill them out.

4. Pair off students in twos. Ask each students to compare and contrast his/her conflict situation with his/her partner.

Discuss (Session One)

1. Did you find any similarities in the kinds of situations each of you experienced? Any differences?

2. Does talking with someone help, even if it is not the person from whom you want to ask forgiveness?

Session Two

1. Explain to the group that you are going to teach them a simple way to resolve conflicts. Using the poster, explain each of the four phases. Here are some important points to cover in your explanation:

Phase One: State the Data

When a person wants to confront another, s/he must first ask to be heard. When the second person agrees to listen, the first person describes what s/he experienced as objectively and clearly as possible.
Example: John, will you listen to me for a moment? (Wait for a "yes" before continuing.) The other day my friends and I were hanging out in the hall when you went to your locker. One of my friends called you a name. We all laughed. He said it again and we laughed harder.

Phase Two: State Your Feelings

Clearly state your feelings. The five most common feelings are mad, sad, glad, afraid, and guilty. When you want to ask forgiveness, you will most likely feel guilty.
Example: At the time I thought it was funny, but then I got to thinking about it and I felt sad. I also felt mad at myself and my friends. Now I am sorry I did that. I feel guilty.

Phase Three: State Your Judgment

It is important to clearly state your judgment or interpretation of the event.
Example: My judgment is that my friends and I were wrong to call you names and laugh. You deserve better than that.

Phase Four: State What You Want

Clearly describe what you want from the other person.
Example: I want you to know I am sorry. I want your respect as a classmate. I want you to know I won't be making fun of you anymore.

2. Ask two students to role play the script provided on page 121. As the actors present the scene, stand at the poster and point to the phase being performed.

3. Ask the students to read the script again, but this time the two students should stop when they finish one of the four phases. Point out to the group how each phase works.

4. Ask the students if they think the conflict between Sue and Mary has been resolved. Can Sue forgive Mary and decide *not* to be friends? What will it take for Sue to trust Mary again?

5. Have the students join the partner from Session One. Ask each pair to create a scene that demonstrates resolving conflict through asking for forgiveness. (See suggestions below.)

6. Ask each pair to perform their example. (If your group is larger than twelve, create groups of twelve in which six demonstrations will be performed.) As each pair performs their scene, ask another student to point to the phases presented using the poster.

7. After each role play, ask the student audience these questions:

Was the role play realistic?

Did the person confronting the other clearly state the data? His/her feelings? His/her judgment? A clear request?

Was the conflict resolved?

Do you have any suggestions for the actors to improve their skills?

Role Play Situations

NOTE: The best role play situations are those identified by the students. Ask them to identify common conflicts, and write their suggestions on a flip chart. Here are some other examples you might want to use:

During a class demonstration, when the teacher is talking, you and a friend have a conversation. The teacher sees your friend talking and gives him/her a detention. The teacher does not see you. You keep you mouth shut and let your friend be punished.

You are with a group that makes insulting remarks to another student.

You promise a friend that you will hang out with her on the weekend, but then you go to the movies with someone else without telling your friend.

A friend tells you that his mom and dad are getting a divorce. He asks you not to tell anyone, but you do. On the bus someone asks your friend if it is true — in front of you both.

Discuss (Session Two)

1. Do you think asking for forgiveness is a good way to talk to someone when you feel you have wronged them in some way?

2. What would make it difficult to use?

3. Is this a better way of handling conflicts or hurtful situations than some other ways you have been using?

4. What makes this a better way?

5. Where in your life can you use this process?

Forgiveness Situation

1. From whom do you need forgiveness?

2. Where were you when the event that you regret took place?

3. What time of day was it?

4. Is this someone you have hurt before?

5. What specifically happened?

6. How do you feel about this situation? Use this scale to indicate how guilty you feel:

   Low   1   2   3   4   5   6   7   High

7. What would you like to do to resolve this situation?

Role Play Script

Mary: Hey, Sue, could I talk with you?

Sue: Sure.

Mary: The other day you told me on the phone that you have a crush on Jake. You told me you hoped he'd ask you out next weekend. You asked me not to tell anyone, but I did. I told Justine and she spread it around. I understand Jake found out.

That made me angry that she did that. Then I realized I had caused a big problem for you and I feel very sorry.

I wanted to be liked by Justine. I used poor judgment. If you had done this to me, I'd be furious.

I want you to forgive me. I hope we can still be friends. I want you to trust me.

Sue: Mary, I was really hurt. I thought I could trust you. I feel you betrayed my friendship, and on top of that now Jake and his buddies know how I feel. I don't know if we can still be friends — I don't know if I can trust you. We'll have to see. I respect you for talking with me and saying you are sorry.

10   Mission Statement Workshop

If you don't know where you want to go,
Any road will take you there.
— AFRICAN-AMERICAN PROVERB

At various times over the course of a lifetime, it is important to define a personal mission — what we want to contribute to make our world and community a better place. Writing a personal mission statement is a valuable culmination to the activities in Part Two, The Personal Journey.

People who have taken the time to develop a mission statement are inspired to make valuable contributions to their lives, the lives of others, and the world in which they live. A mission statement:

- Connects to the deepest personal self, to the principles and values that are held within

- Seeks to express how each person's unique gifts can be used to fulfill the most basic needs in four areas: physical, mental, social, and spiritual

- Inspires excellence

The following sequence of activities is designed to help youth to consider their leadership characteristics, talents they possess, personal roadblocks they are willing to work on, what they individually value in life, and what specific contributions they hope to make. After doing all the following activities in order, participants will be prepared to create a personal mission statement, thereby setting a direction for their present life journey.

Based on the previous experiences in the personal journey so far, here is a sequence of exercises designed to create an inspiring personal mission statement. If you are using these materials in a class, each activity can be accomplished in a class period. In a workshop setting they can be done in a special module.

Personal Dreams

MEDIUM RISK

Purpose

Youth create descriptions of their personal dreams for their future.

Assets Built

#39 Sense of Purpose

#40 Positive View of Personal Future

Materials

8.5×11-inch sheets of paper

pens or pencils

Preparation

1. This activity works best with the participants seated at tables.

2. Select soft music to play as participants write (for example, George Winston, Mozart, or other classical or soft jazz selections).

Activity Instructions

1. Distribute paper and pencils.

2. Ask participants to relax and activate their imaginations.

3. Ask participants to imagine themselves ten or fifteen years in the future. Then ask the following questions:

   Where will you be living?

   Will you be married? Dating? Living alone?

   Will you have children?

   What kind of job will you have? Will you like it?

   Will you be making a lot of money?

   What will you be doing in your spare time?

   What sort of house will you have?

   Who will you know? Old friends? New?

   What kinds of contributions will you be making? To your family?
      To yourself? To your neighborhood or community?

   Will you be happy?

   What will make you happy?

4. Ask participants to create a paragraph — or a set of ten sentences — describing their hopes and dreams for their personal future.

5. Form groups of three to five people each. Ask participants to read their dream descriptions to each other.

6. Ask for volunteers who would like to read their dream descriptions to the group.

Discuss

1. Did anyone's dream vision surprise you?

2. What were some similarities between your vision and those of others? What were some differences?

3. Do you feel you are pursuing this vision now? How? What else might you do to pursue your dreams?

124

What I Value in Life

MEDIUM RISK

Purpose

Youth examine what they value most in life.

Asset Built

#37 Personal Power

Materials

Value Statements worksheet
    (see page 126)

Preparation

Make enough copies of the Value Statements worksheet so each person will have one.

Activity Instructions

1. Distribute the worksheets.

2. Ask participants to think about their positive future.

3. Ask them to examine the value statements on the worksheet. Ask them to rate each statement as of low value, medium value, or high value.

4. Ask participants to place a star by the three things they value the most.

5. Form small groups of three to five for reflective discussion.

Discuss

1. What are the reasons you have selected these values?

2. Do your role models have similar values?

3. Why do you think these values will enrich your life?

Value Statements

Rate the value of the following statements by circling the number that best suits your current position.

Statements	Low						High
Making a lot of money	1	2	3	4	5	6	7
Doing a job I enjoy	1	2	3	4	5	6	7
Doing a job that pays a lot	1	2	3	4	5	6	7
Being admired by others	1	2	3	4	5	6	7
Learning and growing	1	2	3	4	5	6	7
Reaching spiritual fulfillment	1	2	3	4	5	6	7
Building a family	1	2	3	4	5	6	7
Becoming famous	1	2	3	4	5	6	7
Having peace of mind	1	2	3	4	5	6	7
Contributing to others	1	2	3	4	5	6	7
Traveling to far places	1	2	3	4	5	6	7
Being generous to others	1	2	3	4	5	6	7
Being liked by others	1	2	3	4	5	6	7
Having a lot of friends	1	2	3	4	5	6	7

REVIVING THE WONDER WORKSHEET

Characteristics I Admire

MEDIUM RISK

Purpose

Youth identify characteristics of their role models.

Asset Built

#14 Adult Role Models

Materials

Characteristics I Admire worksheet (see page 128) pens or pencils

Preparation

Make enough copies of the Characteristics I Admire worksheet so each person will have one.

Activity Instructions

1. Ask youth to imagine someone (or several people) they know well and admire.

2. Pass out the worksheets. Ask each person to read the list of personal characteristics and check ones they recognize in the people they admire.

3. Ask each person to circle the characteristics that describe him/herself.

4. Ask each person to review the circled characteristics, and then place a star by those (three to five of them) that best describe him/herself.

5. Ask youth to use the blank space on the bottom of the worksheet to list several characteristics they would like to further develop.

Discuss

1. Who did you pick as a role model or a person you admire? Do you know this person or is it someone in the media you have never met?

2. Which specific characteristics do you admire?

3. Which of these do you believe you already possess?

4. What can you do to develop these characteristics?

Characteristics I Admire

_____ Responsible   _____ Leader   _____ Ethical

_____ Respectful   _____ Funny   _____ Patient

_____ Honest   _____ Kind   _____ Intelligent

_____ Laid-back   _____ Educated   _____ Thoughtful

_____ Predictable   _____ Loyal   _____ Fair

_____ Hard working   _____ Independent   _____ Carefree

_____ Decisive   _____ Giving   _____ Healthy

_____ Loving   _____ Wise   _____ Open

_____ Sensitive   _____ Friendly   _____ Jovial

_____ Imaginative   _____ Creative   _____ Moral

_____ Understanding   _____ Sympathetic   _____ Powerful

_____ Committed   _____ Forgiving   _____ Direct

_____ Enthusiastic   _____ Selfless   _____ Balanced

REVIVING THE WONDER WORKSHEET

Strengths Versus Roadblocks

MEDIUM RISK

Purpose

Youth examine the roadblocks in their lives and the strengths they have to overcome those road-blocks.

Asset Built

#37 Personal Power

Materials

Strengths Versus Roadblocks
    worksheet (see page 130)
pens or pencils

Preparation

Make enough copies of the Strengths Versus Roadblocks worksheet so each person will have one.

Activity Instructions

1. Distribute the worksheets.

2. Explain to the participants that roadblocks are negative characteristics that prevent the fulfillment of dreams. These roadblocks can be overcome through the use of character strengths.

3. Ask participants to examine the lists of strengths and roadblocks on the worksheet. Ask them to check three to five of the characteristics they view as their strengths, and up to three roadblocks they are willing to work on and change.

4. Place participants in groups of three to five for reflective discussion.

Discuss

1. What specific evidence can you give that you have these specific strengths?

2. What specific evidence can you give that you have these specific roadblocks?

3. What steps are you willing to take to overcome your roadblocks?

Strengths Versus Roadblocks

Strengths	Roadblocks
_____ Intelligent	_____ Pessimistic
_____ Understanding	_____ Narrow-minded
_____ Optimistic	_____ Unmotivated
_____ Confident	_____ Insecure
_____ Imaginative	_____ Irresponsible
_____ Insightful	_____ Selfish
_____ Hard working	_____ Fearful
_____ Clever	_____ Sarcastic
_____ Artistic	_____ Introverted
_____ Reliable	_____ Bored
_____ Energetic	_____ Vapid
_____ Adaptable	_____ Inflexible
_____ Generous	_____ Impulsive

Contributions I Hope to Make

MEDIUM RISK

Purpose

Youth determine the kinds of contributions they plan to make to their lives, their families, and their communities.

Asset Built

#30 Responsibility

Materials

Contributions I Can Make worksheet (see page 132)
pens or pencils

Preparation

Make enough copies of the Contributions I Can Make worksheet so each person will have one.

Activity Instructions

1. Distribute the worksheets.

2. Ask participants to examine the list of roles on the left side of the worksheet. Suggest that they play many roles now and will in the future.

3. For each area that applies to them personally, ask them to write one specific contribution they can make.

Discuss

1. Do you believe it's possible for a single person or a small group of people to make major changes in the world?

2. What people in your life are making a contribution? What are they doing?

3. What people in the news are making a contribution? What are they doing?

4. Would you like to be in the newspaper or on the cover of a news magazine?

5. Who makes the greater contribution, in your opinion — those who contribute in silence or those who are recognized?

6. Are you aware of any organizations whose purpose it is to make a positive contribution to the community? Would you like to join one?

Contributions I Can Make

Role	Contribution
Daughter or Son	
Friend	
Team Member	
Activity Member	
Student	
Neighbor	
Worker	
Church Member	
Citizen	
Other	

Personal Mission Statement

MEDIUM RISK

Purpose

Youth create a concise mission statement that helps them focus their direction in their life journey.

Assets Built

#30 Responsibility
#39 Sense of Purpose
#40 Positive View of Personal Future

Materials

My Personal Mission worksheet (see page 134)
pens or pencils

Preparation

Make enough copies of the My Personal Mission worksheet so each person will have one.

Activity Instructions

1. Distribute the worksheets.

2. Ask youth to use the work they did on the previous activities in this section to develop their own personal mission statement.

3. Place participants in groups of three to five.

4. Ask them to commit to their mission statements by reading them aloud.

5. Ask for volunteers to read their statements to the large group.

Variation

1. Ask youth to rewrite the mission statement in their own words and then decorate it.

2. Make sure they sign their mission statements.

3. Display the mission statements in a central location.

Discuss

It may be more powerful to simply have the youth read their statements to one another in a small goup. If you want to discuss, here are some questions:

1. What makes these statements powerful?

2. Do any of the statements surprise you?

3. How often do you think you ought to look at your statements in the future?

4. When do you think you ought to revise your statements?

5. Would you recommend this experience to others?

My Personal Mission

I want to live a positive life, fulfill my dreams, and contribute to making this world a better place. In order to do this I will...

1. Seek to fulfill the following dreams during my lifetime:

2. Value each of the following:

3. Develop the following characteristics I admire in others:

4. Use my strengths and increase my talents:

5. Work on overcoming these roadblocks:

6. Seek to make the following contributions in the roles I live:

PART THREE

Transformations

The journey in between what you once were and who you are
now becoming is where the dance of life really takes place.

— BARBARA DE ANGELIS

Night follows day; day follows night. Season moves into season in subtle cycles. In our lives each of us moves from season to season: from womb to birth to childhood to adolescence to adulthood to middle age to elder to death.

During the life journey, each of us makes transformations from one time in our life to another. At each of these cusps or transition times, the transition is eased if the initiates are welcomed, honored, and initiated by those who have already made the transition. In this sense, initiation includes six important components:

- The person making the transition is given a clear understanding, both directly and indirectly, that the initiate is making a passage.

- The journey is important and necessary.

- Help and guidance are available.

- A community is ready to receive the initiate as a full member.

- There is necessary work to be done that is specifically related to making the passage.

- New responsibilities are expected of all who enter this new stage in life.

Part One, Optimum Learning Environments, describes how to create an optimum learning environment in which adults and youth can meaningfully work together. Part Two, The Personal Journey, presents ways youth can get in touch with their inner spirit; understand their personal values, principles, and beliefs; identify role models; make connections with others; and create a positive mission for themselves. Part Three helps adults guide youth into an understanding of themselves as growing men and women. Included in this part are a sequence of activities that can be used to create acts of stewardship or service and a rite of initiation or passage that reflects the community's specific heritage, principles, values, and beliefs.

The work boys and girls need to do to make the passage from childhood to adulthood includes coming to an understanding of themselves as growing men and women, how their community defines the roles of each, how each ought to treat others, what rights and responsibilities youth have as they become adults, and how they might take on meaningful stewardship or service as a response to the needs of their community.

By considering how men and women differ and how they are alike, youth come to a clearer understanding of who they are. Through relationships with role model adults, youth are given support and guidance. By creating a code of ethics and conduct between the sexes, youth and adults create a community where boys and girls grow into mature men and women with a clearer understanding of how they might live together.

When youth are honored by the adults in their community as they pass into adulthood in a formal way, the confusion about where they are headed is lifted. They are no longer separated from the adults in their community. They are given guidance and support, and they more freely and openly take on the responsibilities of adulthood.

Finally, when youth are given the opportunity to serve in meaningful ways, they take on these new responsibilities with help and guidance. In this way, they move from self-centeredness to group and community awareness, taking ownership of their heritage as they make a difference in the life of their community.

11 Girl into Woman, Boy into Man

I say to the young: Do not stop thinking of life as an adventure.
You have no security unless you can live bravely, excitingly,
imaginatively.

— ELEANOR ROOSEVELT

The following activities are designed with the specific intent that boys and girls will use them to identify and clarify their ideas about gender — the ideas they have about their own gender and those they hold about the opposite sex. Because our culture has rapidly changed the roles each sex plays and because many ideas change from community to community, it is important that these activities be conducted with honor and integrity.

A critical key to successful work in this area is connecting youth with adult role models who are willing to speak of their own experiences and who are willing to mentor youth in this area. Try to find a large number of adults from the community who represent many age groups and walks of life.

The activities follow a deliberate sequence:

1. Examination of cultural images, myths, and expectations

2. Creation of useful definitions of gender

3. Examination of how each gender treats the other

4. Creation of a code of ethics individuals in the group can use as guidelines for their community or school

Throughout these activities, the overriding goal is that the tension between the sexes will relax and that a clearer understanding of appropriate behavior will emerge.

Ideas About Men and Women

LOW RISK

Purpose

Youth examine their notions of masculinity and femininity, and compare their ideas with those of the opposite sex.

Asset Built

#34 Cultural Competence

Materials

two large sheets of paper
color markers

Sample Questions

What words do you generally use to describe men? To describe women?

What activities do you generally think of as masculine? As feminine?

What interests do you usually associate with men? With women?

What specific ways do men act, feel, or think? What specific ways do women act, feel, or think?

Preparation

1. This activity works best when you can separate the sexes so boys and girls are working in two different rooms. If this is not possible, use opposite sides of the room so that people in one group can focus on the drawings and not see or hear the other group.

2. Draw stylized illustrations of a male form and a female form on each of the two sheets of paper (four feet by six feet) to make two identical posters with both the male and the female forms.

3. Tape one poster on a wall for the girls group, the other on a wall for the boys group.

Activity Instructions

1. Separate the youth into same-sex groups.

2. Select a facilitator for each group who will record the group's suggestions on the poster.

3. Ask each group to generate a list of words and phrases associated with men and and a second list of words and phrases associated with women. Sample questions you may want to ask to elicit responses are shown to the left.

4. Bring groups back together as one and examine both posters together.

Discuss

1. Did both groups come up with the same words for each sex? Were there any differences?

2. Could any of the words and phrases associated with one sex also apply to the other?

3. What is the origin of these notions of masculine and feminine?

4. If a boy or a girl associates with a word or phrase from the opposite sex, how do you react?

5. Are there any words or phrases that should apply to only one sex?

Media Images

LOW RISK

Purpose

Youth examine the images of men and women projected by the media.

Asset Built

#34 Cultural Competence

Materials

magazines
newspapers
videotapes
television
video cassette recorder
blackboard or whiteboard
chalk or color markers

Preparation

1. This activity works best in an ongoing class situation rather than in a one-time-only workshop.

2. Make collections of images of men and women found in newspaper and magazine advertisements and on television.

3. Divide the display area of a blackboard, whiteboard, or large sheet of paper into the following categories:

   How Men Should Look, Act, Think, and Feel

   How Women Should Look, Act, Think, and Feel

Activity Instructions

1. Form groups of four to six participants.

2. Allow each small group to examine the collected advertisements and commercials.

3. Reassemble as a large group.

4. Challenge youth to list the ways — according to what they have seen in the ads — men and women should look, act, think, and feel.

Discuss

1. Are specific types of men and women portrayed in the media?

2. What specific messages are hidden behind the product advertisement about how men and women ought to look? Act? Behave?

3. In the advertisements, are specific types of work or play associated with one sex or the other?

4. Are these images realistic?

5. How are you affected by these images?

6. Do people you consider to be popular and/or successful fit these media images?

7. Do you try to fit these images by purchasing the advertised products? By wearing the styles portrayed? By acting the way you see people act in the advertisements?

Model Interview

LOW RISK

Purpose

Youth interview male and female print and TV models to see if how they look and the lives they lead are similar to or different from the images they project in the media.

Asset Built

#34 Cultural Competence

Materials

photographs and video ads from a modeling agency
paper and pens
tape recorder and cassette tapes

Preparation

1. Contact a local modeling agency. Invite several male and female models to come for an interview.

2. Ask the agency to send copies of posed pictures and of print and video ads in which the models have appeared.

Activity Instructions

1. Pass out paper and pens. Working with the group, prepare a set of questions you would like to ask the models. Sample questions:

    Questions About Being a Model
    Why did you want to become a model?
    What did you have to do to become a model?
    What is modeling work like?

    Questions About Their Real Life
    How is your life similar to the images you portray in ads?
    How is your life different from the images you portray?

2. Introduce the panel of models.

3. Set up the tape recorder to record the interview.

4. Ask the models questions that will elicit information about their lives as models and about their real lives.

Discuss

1. What images of males are projected by the models' photographs and advertisements? What images of females?

2. How is the real life of the models similar to the images they project in their photographs and advertisements? How is their real life different?

Gender Differences

LOW RISK

Purpose

Youth consider the differences between the genders.

Asset Built

#34 Cultural Competence

Materials

newsprint (eight large sheets)
color markers

Preparation

1. This activity works well when groups can go to separate rooms. If that is not possible, create two work areas apart from each other.

2. Tape up four large sheets of newsprint in each work area.

3. Label four distinct areas for recording responses, one on each sheet of newsprint:
   Physical
   Mental
   Social
   Spiritual

Activity Instructions

1. Separate into same-sex groups.

2. Ask each group to choose a recorder.

3. Ask youth to consider the four areas, then brainstorm ways the group feels the opposite sex differs from them in each area.

4. Ask the recorder to write the responses on the sheets of newsprint.

5. Reassemble as a large group.

6. Post the results of both groups.

Discuss

1. Are there more similarities or differences?

2. Are there surprising similarities? Surprising differences?

3. Circle those items that represent real differences you perceive between the genders.

Question Cards

Purpose

Youth and elders create questions they want to ask one another. Youth often want to know what growing up was like for adults and what they learned from their life experiences. Adults often want to understand the youth culture. This panel discussion offers youth and adults the opportunity to question each other.

Asset Built

#33 Interpersonal Competence

Materials

3×5-inch index cards
pens or pencils
two boxes with lids
portable microphone (for large groups)

Preparation

1. Select a panel of four to six adults and four to six youth who are willing to answer questions posed to them by an audience.

2. Create two question boxes — one for youth, one for adults. Shoeboxes work well. Cut a hole in the lid through which a 3×5-inch index card can fit. Label the two boxes:
    Questions for Youth
    Questions for Adults

3. Arrange the room with two long tables in the front for the two panel members — one for youth and one for adults. For large groups, you might need a portable microphone for the panel discussion.

Activity Instructions

1. Distribute index cards and pens or pencils to the participants.

2. Ask participants to write one question per card.

3. Tell adults to put their question cards in the "Questions for Youth" box.

4. Tell youth to put their question cards in the "Questions for Adults" box.

5. Ask the panel members to come forward and introduce them to the audience.

6. Select a moderator. The moderator pulls one question card out of the box at a time, alternating boxes, and addresses the question to the appropriate panel.

7. Allow for follow-up questions.

Some Tips About Questions

1. Encourage a wide range of questions.

2. Do not limit the subjects.

3. Watch for "permission questions." Permission questions are usually questions youth ask when they are seeking permission to engage in some activity.

    Example:
    "Is it okay to drink at a friend's home if you're not going to drive?"

Adults might need to be coached to answer permission questions this way: "You will have to make your own decisions based on your own moral and ethical code, your family's values, and your personal convictions. It helps to clearly understand your values when you make these decisions. Be sure you discuss these decisions with adults who are important in your life."

4. The appropriate answer to any question that asks for the disclosure of personal experiences is a matter of personal choice for the person asked.

Discuss

1. Which of the topics discussed did you find most relevant to you and your life?

2. Which were the most compelling?

3. Which answers were the most intriguing? What information did you acquire that you will find useful?

4. Do you think the answers given were practical?

Situation Cards

Purpose

Youth and adults create situations pertaining to personal responsibilities, then role-play and discuss the most appropriate behavior.

Asset Built

#30 Responsibility

Materials

5×8-inch index cards
pens or pencils

Activity Instructions

1. Create random groups of youth and adults, eight to twelve per group.

2. Distribute index cards and pencils or pens.

3. Ask groups to create problem situations according to the area you suggest. Be sure that situations are realistic and relevant to the problems of youth in your group. Possible areas to suggest:

   Dating
   Friendships
   Relationships between parents and youth
   Relationships within a clique
   Relationships among several different cliques
   Work
   School
   Balancing school, work, and other activities
   Being honest
   Decisions about sex
   Decisions about drinking

A situation card might read like this:

A junior student/athlete hopes to attend college and play sports at the collegiate level. His teachers are suggesting more study time and a tutor to improve his grades. He has taken a job to earn money to date and buy clothes. His girlfriend wants to see him more often. His coach has recommended a more strenuous exercise program and practice schedule. His other friends wonder why they don't see him and want him to hang out with them. Lately, his grades have slipped, his girlfriend has suggested she might be interested in dating other guys, his friends have stopped calling, and his parents want to talk with him about his grades.

4. At this point, you have two options for continuing with the activity.

Option 1

1. Place all the situation cards in a box.

2. Ask each small group to draw a situation card to consider. They may not use the situation they created.

3. Ask each small group to consider the situation and suggest three to five positive solutions.

4. Ask each team to present the situation and its solutions to the larger group.

Discuss (for Option 1)

1. Is the problem you solved realistic? Is this a common problem? Have you ever been in a similar situation?

2. List the solutions on a flip chart. Are there any other options? (Solutions to different problems will often be the same.) Circle solutions that are realistic and possible to do, and that will resolve the dilemma.

Option 2

1. Place all the situation cards in a box.

2. Each small group draws a situation card to consider. They may not use the situation they created.

3. Ask each small group to create a skit presenting the dilemma and possible solutions.

4. Follow each skit with a discussion of the issue presented.

Discuss (for Option 2)

1. Did you understand the situation? Who can summarize the situation and suggest what the problem is?

2. Do problems like this happen? Has anyone been in a situation like this? What happened?

3. List on the board or on a flip chart all the positive solutions offered.

4. Circle the solutions that are realistic, possible to do, and that will resolve the dilemma.

Fishbowl

MEDIUM RISK

Purpose

Same-sex groups hear what the opposite sex wants them to know that they don't seem to know.

Asset Built

#34 Cultural Competence

Materials

no materials necessary

Fishbowl Metaphor

Those observing fish in an aquarium can see the fish, but the fish are oblivious to the observers. Likewise, during the fishbowl activity, the observers can see and hear those inside the fishbowl. Those inside the fishbowl carry on a conversation as though they were alone. Those outside the fishbowl may not speak, comment, ask questions, or talk among themselves.

Preparation

1. In the center of the room, set up an inner circle and an outer circle of chairs, enough chairs so each person will have one.

2. This activity works best in a large room with good acoustics.

Activity Instructions

1. Select youth and adults of the same sex to sit in the chairs in the center of the room. These are the fish in the fishbowl.

2. Ask all others to sit around the outer circle of chairs. These are the observers on the outside of the fishbowl, looking in.

3. Pose the question to the fish: "What do you wish the opposite sex knew about you that they do not seem to know?" You can rephrase the question in a variety of ways:

   What do you wish the opposite sex knew about you?

   What is it about your gender that they don't seem to know?

   What does the opposite sex need to know about you that would make your life easier?

   Ask those inside the fishbowl to respond only for themselves, not as representatives of their group (i.e., their gender).

4. Allow five to fifteen minutes for the fish to generate possible answers to the question. When answers become repetitious, call time.

5. Invite the youth and elders of the opposite sex to sit in the fishbowl. Pose the same questions.

Discuss

Ask the following questions of the large group, both sexes mixed together:

1. Was the discussion realistic?

2. Did it answer any questions for you?

3. Do you think people were being honest?

4. What did you learn that was new?

5. How can you apply what you learned?

How We'd Like to Be Treated

MEDIUM RISK

Purpose

Youth suggest through skits how they'd like to be treated by the opposite sex.

Asset Built

#27 Equality and Social Justice

Materials

List of appropriate situations for groups to consider as subject matter for skits.

Sample Situations

During class
During lunch period
At the mall
At school events
In the neighborhood
In the community
On a date

Preparation

This activity runs smoother when you can use two separate rooms. If that is not possible, create separate areas within a large room.

Activity Instructions

1. Separate into same-sex groups.

2. Suggest to the groups a number of situations to consider. See Sample Situations (to the left).

3. Ask each group to discuss ways they'd like to be treated by the opposite sex in each situation.

4. Ask groups to put together skits to depict how they would like to be treated by the opposite sex in each situation. Skits should be no longer than five minutes.

5. Each group performs skits for the opposite sex group. Alternate presentation of skits, so that the girls' and boys' skits on the same situation come one after the other. For example, the girls do their "At the Mall" skit, then the boys do their "At the Mall" skit. Also alternate which sex goes first.

Variation

In large groups of more than forty participants, separate into same-sex groups of eight to twelve people, and give each group one or two specific situations (each group gets different situations).

Discuss

1. What did you learn? Was it surprising?

2. For any situations presented, does the way you treat each other now differ? If so, which is better?

3. How realistic were the skits? Was the behavior depicted doable in real life?

4. How can you apply what you learned to real life?

Elder Circle

MEDIUM RISK

Purpose

Youth hear from elders concerning the passage from youth to adulthood.

Assets Built

#3   Other Adult Relationships
#14 Adult Role Models

Materials

no materials necessary

Preparations

1. Invite a minimum of seven adults; fifteen to twenty work well. Invite several from different age groups — twenty-one to thirty, thirty-one to forty, forty-one to fifty, over fifty.

2. Set up a circle of chairs in the center of the room.

3. Provide one chair per elder.

Activity Instructions

1. Ask the group of elders to sit in the chairs.

2. Ask youth to sit around the elders so they can hear.

3. Caution youth to listen, maintain silence, and avoid side comments. Tell them questions can be asked at the end of each session.

4. Ask the elder circle to discuss the questions that are relevant for the group of youth and their community. Consider asking one question at a time before going on to the next one. Sample questions:

   What do you know now that you wish you knew when you were younger?

   In what ways were you initiated as a youth into the adult culture? School? Military service? Religious ceremony? Relationships with older members of the community?

   What did you learn from that initiation?

   What rights and responsibilities do you have as an adult?

   Do your rights and responsibilities differ from those of the opposite sex?

   How do you know you are a man? A woman?

5. Allow youth to ask questions of the elders.

Discuss

1. Do you think the elders are in touch with today's youth?

2. Which of the responses was most interesting? Useful? Practical?

3. Did you hear anything that might change an opinion you hold?

4. Who among the elders would you ask for advice?

5. Are there any questions left unanswered? If so, where would you go to find the answers?

What Does Respect Look Like?

MEDIUM RISK

Purpose

Youth describe in specific detail what it would look like if boys and girls respected one another.

Asset Built

#12 School Boundaries

Materials

flip chart

poster board (one)

color markers

Preparation

On a flip-chart sheet, write in large letters the following questions for the group to consider:

> What would it look like if males and females respected each other?

> What specifically would you see and hear?

Post this so everyone can read the questions.

Activity Instructions

1. Select a recorder to record responses on the flip chart.

2. Post the two questions and ask the group to imagine respectful relations between the sexes.

3. Facilitate a discussion of the above questions. In addition, examine the overriding question of whether males and females should be treated differently.

4. Recorder writes down all responses.

5. When the group runs out of answers, examine the list created.

6. Ask the group, "Which of these behaviors could you do at school? In your neighborhood? At school functions? Throughout your life?"

7. Circle or mark in some way those responses the group would be willing to perform at school.

8. Ask for one or two volunteers to rewrite the circled responses neatly on a large poster-size piece of paper.

9. Suggest these statements as a code of ethics for the group to follow. Ask each person to sign this code of ethics at the bottom of the poster.

10. Display the poster at a central location.

Discuss

After this activity, periodically check in with the group to see how they feel they are doing in living up to their code of ethics.

1. Are you following the code as it was intended?

2. What parts of this code are you following?

3. In what areas do you need to make changes?

4. What difference has following this code made in your community?

Separate Tables

Purpose

Youth discuss in same-sex groups their experiences as a member of that sex.

Asset Built

#34 Cultural Competence

Materials

no materials necessary

Preparation

1. This activity works well with groups sitting at tables, in circles of chairs, or in circles on the floor.

2. If you are working with a small group (fifteen or fewer), see Variation on page 151.

Activity Instructions

1. Separate the boys from the girls on each side of the room.

2. Form same-sex groups of three to eight. Seat each group at a table or in a circle (on chairs or on the floor).

3. Tell the groups you are going to give them a topic to discuss. Warn them that they will be reporting their findings to the larger group.

4. Use this pattern:

   Pose a question.

   Let groups discuss the question for one to five minutes.

   Ask each group to select one person to report to the large group.

   Pose a second question.

   Let groups discuss the question for one to five minutes.

   Ask each group to select a different person to report to the large group.

   Repeat for a total of six rounds.

5. Here are the questions:

   Round 1   What are the coolest things about the sex you are?

   Round 2   What are the most difficult things about being a girl (a boy)?

   Round 3   What are the most confusing things about being a girl (a boy)?

   Round 4   What is it about the opposite sex you would find cool if you were that sex?

   Round 5   What is it about the opposite sex you would find difficult if you were that sex?

   Round 6   What is it about the opposite sex you would find confusing if you were that sex?

6. Bring the groups back together in one large group for discussions (questions on the next page).

Discuss

1. What similarities did you find between the sexes? What differences?

2. Do you have a better understanding of the other sex?

3. Did any of the answers surprise you?

4. Did you learn something that might make it easier to communicate with the opposite sex?

5. Why do you think understanding and communicating with the opposite sex is sometimes difficult?

Variation

If you are working with a small group of fifteen or fewer participants, have them sit in a circle, alternating males and females in the circle. Ask one sex to listen without comment while the other discusses each round. Use the discussion rounds on page 150 and the discussion questions above.

Personal Boundaries

MEDIUM RISK

Purpose

Youth identify their personal boundaries.

Asset Built

#33 Interpersonal Competence

Materials

large paper banners (two)
poster board
color markers

Preparation

Cut two six-foot-long paper banners. Draw stylized forms of a boy and a girl, one on each banner.

Activity Instructions

1. Select a recorder to record suggestions from the group.

2. Discuss the meanings of boundaries and why they are important so that people know what to expect from one another.

3. Take suggestions from the group and list on the banners a set of boundaries they would set for each other. Examples:

    Refrain from spreading gossip and rumors.

    When you are in conflict with someone, first go to that person to try to resolve the problem.

    Don't tell jokes that hurt feelings.

4. Circle those boundaries the group accepts.

5. Make a poster of the agreed-upon boundaries.

6. Ask each person to sign off on the boundaries they set.

7. Display the poster at a central location.

Discuss

1. Are these boundaries realistic and possible to achieve?

2. Are there any personal boundaries between opposite-sex friendships that are different from the personal boundaries between same-sex friendships?

Personal Banners

MEDIUM RISK

Purpose

Youth create banners to portray "Myself As a Man" or "Myself As a Woman."

Asset Built

#39 Sense of Purpose

Materials

paper banners (two six-foot-long banners per person)
color markers
masking tape

Preparation

Cut two six-foot-long banners for each participant.

Activity Instructions

1. Divide large group into same-sex groups.

2. Distribute markers and banners.

3. Ask each person to create a banner that reflects his/her essential essence as a person. Banners should include:

   Personal role models
   Feminine (or masculine) characteristics I possess that I like
   Gifts I have to give others
   Personal dreams
   Work I'd like to do
   Personal motto
   What I bring to relationships
   Personal code of ethics

4. Create a gallery of personal banners by taping them up around the room. Next to each person's banner, tape up a blank banner with only the participant's name at the top.

5. Ask the group to move around the room and view the personal banners. Then ask them to write positive comments on the blank banners.

Discuss

1. Did you discover anything new about the people in the group?

2. Were you surprised by any of the comments people wrote to and about you?

3. How did these comments make you feel?

Variation

Personal Mailboxes

1. Give each participant a blank 9×12-inch envelope.

2. Ask each person to decorate his/her envelope with words and symbols that reflect who s/he is as a person.

3. Supply participants with small sheets of paper and pencils.

4. Ask participants to write positive notes to each other.

5. Hang up the envelopes and use them as personal mailboxes.

Game of Life

Purpose

Youth and elders consider the essential knowledge every youth ought to have by age eighteen.

Asset Built

#37 Personal Power

Materials

flip chart or newsprint

scissors

rulers

pencils

poster board (one piece per small group)

color markers

construction paper

white school glue

3×5-inch colored index cards, one pack of 100 cards per group

dice (one pair per group)

Preparation

1. This activity works best with groups of six to eight, seated around large tables.

2. In a central location, set up a supply table with all the materials listed.

3. Each group will need a flip chart or a large sheet of newsprint.

Activity Instructions

Part 1

1. Divide participants into small groups that combine six to eight youth and adults.

2. Ask each group to select a recorder.

3. Ask each group to discuss possible answers to the basic theme question: "What should every youth know by the age of eighteen?"

4. Ask the recorder in each group to write down the final suggestions of the group on the newsprint or flip chart.

5. Have each group post its sheet on the wall by its work table.

6. Ask each group to create a board game using the poster board and art materials from the materials table. The game must reflect the group's answers listed on the newsprint. Here are some suggestions:

   Games in which participants must take a journey from one part of the board to another, moving space by space, work well.

   Spaces with typical problems work well.
   Example: You flunk a test at school. Lose one turn.

   Spaces with rewards work well.
   Example: You get your first job. Move three spaces forward.

   Questions should reflect the theme of what one ought to know to survive by age eighteen.
   Example:
   Question: Along with a job application, what kind of letter might you have to provide a possible employer?
   Answer: A reference letter.

Make it obligatory to answer questions in order to move. Write a question on one side of a card, the answer on the other. Opposing teams can pose the questions.

Example: If you answer one of the questions correctly, you can roll the dice and move that number of spaces.

Most groups of youth are very clever at creating these games and often invent games that are ingenious. Forty-five minutes to an hour is usually sufficient to create the game.

Part 2

1. Ask each group to set up its game for play.

2. Create a pattern for groups to move easily about the room from game to game. Moving either clockwise or counterclockwise works well.

3. Allow five to ten minutes per game. (This may only give them a taste of each game in a forty-five minute period.)

4. One or two persons per group must stay with the game to explain how it works. The "explainers" can be changed each round.

5. Groups rotate until all the groups play all the games.

Discuss

1. Which games did you enjoy playing?

2. Did you learn anything new?

3. If you had a son or daughter, what essential facts about life would you want him/her to know? How would you separate "facts" from "opinions"?

4. If you are confused about what you should know by the time you are eighteen, who should you ask?

12   Stewardship

*Service is the rent we pay for living. It is the very purpose of life
and not something you do in your spare time.*

— MARIAN WRIGHT EDELMAN

Stewardship means giving time, talent, and treasure to create and implement service to the community. Young people are able to clearly indicate their desire to serve in meaningful ways. Most want to be an integral part of the entire process and they want to make a difference. Those who work in the area of service need to encourage students to create meaningful service projects, help them reflect on their experiences during the service time, and celebrate their successes as their projects come to a close.

In this chapter, the movement is from creating a vision for the school or community toward specific action plans for specific projects. During the entire process, youth engaged in these activities will develop skills for living as well as skills to use in giving service.

Card Castles

MEDIUM RISK

Purpose

Through use of a metaphor, youth learn how to develop a stewardship plan.

Asset Built

#33 Interpersonal Competence

Materials

5×8-inch index cards, 300 to 500, of many colors

Preparation

1. This activity works best in a large room without furniture.

2. The more time and the more cards the participants have, the more elaborate the structures will become.

Activity Instructions

1. Create small groups of eight to twelve people.

2. Give these instructions:

   Your task is to create a structure or castle at least ten stories high. In addition, you must connect your castle to three other castles using cards to make roads and bridges.

   You can fold the cards in the middle widthwise — like this (show them a model). Please do not fold, spindle, or mutilate the cards in any other way.

   Use all the cards you are given. There are no other cards available.

   Any questions?

   This will be a silent activity. From this point on no talking, please. If you have a question, please raise your hand. I will come to you and quietly answer your question. Please remain silent until I give a signal to speak.

   Begin.

3. Allow about twenty minutes for the building of the castles.

Discuss

1. What did you learn?

2. Was it difficult or helpful working in silence?

3. What did you learn about communication? About teamwork?

4. When you stood back and looked at the whole area, were you surprised? What did you notice? What thoughts do you have when you look at the castle village?

5. How is this activity like life?

Adapted from "Card Castles," Michelle Karns, *How to Create Positive Relationships with Students: A Handbook of Group Activities and Teaching Strategies* (Champaign, IL: Research Press, 1994), p. 129.

Build Me a World

MEDIUM RISK

Purpose

Youth create a description of the most desirable future they can imagine.

Asset Built

#40 Positive View of Personal Future

Materials

flip charts or large sheets of newsprint

color markers

Preparation

If you are working with more than twenty-five people, create groups of eight to twelve. Divide the room into work areas for each group.

Activity Instructions

1. Challenge each group to create a series of sentences that describe the most ideal world ten years from now. Examples:

   There is world peace.

   All people are well fed.

   All people have clean drinking water.

2. You might want to limit the number of statements to ten or fifteen.

Discuss

1. How realistic is your ideal world?

2. Which of these goals do you now enjoy in your local community?

3. Which of these goals could you affect by your actions now?

Ideal School

MEDIUM RISK

Purpose

Youth are challenged to create a compelling vision for stewardship planning.

Asset Built

#5   Caring School Climate

Materials

flip chart (one per group)
legal notepad (one per group)
color markers
pens

Activity Instructions

1. Tell participants they are going to take an imaginary tour of the school. Suggest that their school has been selected as an example of a school where outstanding learning takes place, where student-teacher relationships are strong, where student-to-student relationships are supportive, and where both students and teachers love to come to school. The tour will last one day.

2. To begin, ask them to relax, close their eyes, and imagine the following:

   You arrive at school in the morning just before school opens. What do you see and hear? The students are arriving. What's happening?

   Notice the outside of the school grounds and the front of the building. What do you notice?

   As you enter the school, what do you notice about the internal environment? What's happening in the halls?

   You enter several classrooms. Describe the teaching and the learning. How do the students and teachers interact?

   You enter the teacher's lounge. What's happening?

   School ends. Where do the students go? What happens?

   Examine several activities. What's going on? Describe the interaction between activity leader and youth.

   It's evening. What meetings are happening? Who attends? What happens?

3. Form small groups for reflective discussion.

4. Ask each group to choose a recorder who will write down the ideas generated by the discussion questions.

Discuss

1. What would be essential in the ideal school?

2. What would you see, hear, feel?

3. How well does your school match the school you imagined?

4. What changes could you make at your school to make it more "ideal"?

Adapted with permission from Steven L. Zuieback, *Facilitating Community Partnerships* (Sebastopol, CA: National Training Associates, undated), p. 84. *Facilitating Community Partnerships* was developed with assistance from a grant from California Community Colleges.

Ideal School Chart

MEDIUM RISK

Purpose

Youth develop ideas they have for an ideal school.

Asset Built

#5   Caring School Climate

Materials

newsprint or flip-chart paper
(one sheet per topic)
color markers
masking tape

Preparation

1. At the top of each sheet of paper, write the topics you have selected for brainstorming. Sample topics:

   Student-to-student relationships

   Teacher-to-student relationships

   Administration

   Courses Offered

   Extracurricular activities

   After-school programs

   School functions

   Student government

2. Hang the sheets around the room.

3. Create a workstation at each sheet of paper. Each station will need markers and a circle of chairs.

Activity Instructions

A small group can move together from chart to chart. For more than ten, create smaller groups and assign one to each workstation.

1. Ask the participants to brainstorm ideas under each topic to create the ideal school in that area.

2. Have each group choose a recorder who writes down the ideas and presents them to the large group.

Discuss

1. Examine and circle the ideas that can easily be implemented.

2. Place a star next to the ideas that will take a special project.

3. Underline the ideas that are extremely difficult or unrealistic.

4. From among all the recorded actions, ask the people to determine which (three to five) are the most compelling actions the group wants to work on. Record these ideas to use for later planning.

Keep, Change, and Build

MEDIUM RISK

Purpose

Youth consider which aspects about their school they'd like to keep, which aspects they'd like to change, and new programs they'd like to create.

Assets Built

#24 Bonding to School
#32 Planning and Decision
       Making

Materials

3 flip charts, 3 large sheets of
    newsprint, or 3 sections of a
    blackboard
color markers or color chalk

Preparation

On each of the large sheets, print in large letters one of the following:

KEEP: Things about our school we really like and want to build upon.

CHANGE: Things about our school we really dislike and want to change.

BUILD: New ideas and programs we'd like to see created or built.

Activity Instructions

1. Introduce the three categories (keep, change, build) to the group.

2. Select three recorders.

3. Facilitate a brainstorming session with the group. Ask them to identify ideas, behaviors, programs, and attitudes they'd like to keep, change, or build. Examples:

KEEP	Positive relationships with staff
	Great selection of courses
	Fun and exciting after-school activities
CHANGE	Fights among cliques
	Boring classes
	Limited activities
BUILD	More peaceful relationships between the sexes
	An intramural sports program
	New foreign language offerings

4. Have the recorders write down all the answers on the appropriate sheet.

5. Examine all the suggestions under "Change" and "Build."

6. Place a star next to any suggestions that can be easily achieved. Underline those that will take a special project to accomplish. Circle those that appear extremely difficult to implement.

7. From among all the recorded changes and ideas for building, ask the people to determine which (three to five) are the most compelling actions the group wants to work on. Record these ideas to later use for planning.

Action Planning

MEDIUM RISK

Purpose

Youth create a set of action plans to implement their vision.

Assets Built

#24 Bonding to School
#32 Planning and Decision Making

Materials

Action Plan worksheet (see page 164)
pens or pencils
file folders

Preparation

Make three to five copies of the Action Plan worksheet per small group.

Activity Instructions

1. Examine the results of the following activities: Ideal School (page 160), Ideal School Chart (page 161), Keep, Change, and Build (page 162).

2. Make a list of specific activities to which the group is willing to commit time and energy to complete.

3. Ask participants to select several activities they would like to work on.

4. Create small groups of no more than fifteen to plan a specific activity.

5. Ask each group to create an action plan using the form provided as a worksheet.

    Project description: This should be a detailed description that includes what and why.

    Completion date: Each activity should take no more than ninety days to complete.

    Captain: Name of person who will oversee the entire project.

    Team members: Names of those supporting and working on the project.

    Steps: Describe every step necessary to complete the project.

    Who: Name the person responsible for doing and/or overseeing this step.

    When: Date that step must be completed.

Discuss

1. Do you have a good description of the project?

2. Have you anticipated all the steps necessary to complete the project?

3. Do you have a person responsible for each step?

4. Are the due dates reasonable?

5. Do you need anyone's help or support who is not in the group?

6. For each step, from whom do you need approval?

7. When will the group meet again?

Action Plan

Project description:

Completion date: Captain:

Team members:

Steps	Who?	When?	Remarks
1.			
2.			
3.			
4.			
5.			
6.			
7.			

Peace Quilt

MEDIUM RISK

Purpose

Youth identify specific projects they can act upon on a regular basis to make the world, the school, and the community a better place.

Asset Built

#30 Responsibility

Materials

8.5×11-inch color sheets of paper
color markers
masking tape
large blank wall
flip-chart paper or newsprint

Preparation

1. On a flip chart or large piece of newsprint, print the following:

   In order to make the world and my school [or my community] a better place, I [facilitator's name], will

   1. [specific action]
   2. [specific action]
   3. [specific action]

   Your "action plan" will become a model for others. Post it in a central location so all can see.

2. Select three or four different pastel colors of paper to use. Each participant will need one sheet and several markers.

3. Following steps 2–4 in the Activity Instructions below, create a sample quilt piece.

4. Clear a wall to use for assembling the paper quilt.

Activity Instructions

1. Ask participants to consider simple actions they can take on a regular basis to make their school or community a better place. Examples:

   One day each week, I will invite someone new to my lunch table.

   One day each week, I will help a teacher clean his/her classroom.

2. Pass out 8.5×11-inch paper and markers to everyone.

3. Show the group your sample quilt piece to demonstrate the activity.

4. Ask participants to copy the words from the newsprint onto their 8.5×11-inch sheets (but not your specific actions), adding their names and up to three actions they are willing to do to make their school or community a better place. Ask them to make sure the actions are specific, achievable, and regular.

5. After they have written their actions, ask them to decorate their quilt pieces.

6. Distribute tape and ask participants to place four loops of tape in the four corners of the back on their pieces.

7. Ask each youth to read his piece to the group and place it on the wall to form the peace quilt.

8. Explain that if each of us does these simple things, we can increase peace and harmony in our small world — and the world at large.

Discuss

1. What do you think will happen to your school or community if everyone performs the actions they have said they will?

2. What will be difficult?

3. How can we help each other keep our commitments?

13   Rites of Passage and Initiation

How many of our sons go through a second birth into manhood that is guided and honored by families, communities, the society as a whole as a spiritual passage, central to the welfare of the boy, his family, community, and culture?

— MICHAEL GURIAN

Throughout life, each individual makes transitions from one phase to another — from infancy to childhood, from childhood to adolescence, from adolescence to adulthood. Each transition is marked by an initiation. Sometimes transitions are formally marked, often through a formal ceremony that celebrates the change. At other times the marking is informal, even accidental. Formal or informal, the transition into a new phase brings about new and different feelings and actions.

In *The Wonder of Boys,* Michael Gurian defines five types of initiation or rites of passage:[1]

Planned	Passing the test for a driver's license
Institutional	Bar Mitzvah, Bat Mitzvah, graduation day
Accidental	First date, first kiss
Incidental	Victory within the context of a larger structure like sports or the workplace: scoring a winning basket, being awarded a promotion, winning a contest
Ritual	Formal ritual (for example, a church ceremony, or a Vision Quest) with four distinctive components:

> Safe place
>
> Trusted elders
>
> Prepared ritual accepted by the community
>
> Ritual imbued with sacred energy and tradition

Many commentators and social scientists have suggested that a lack of formal initiation of children into the adult society is a cause of many of the social woes we currently face with youth, including the forming of violent gangs among youth who are disconnected from their elders. Harvard anthropologist Carlton Coon writes about this in *The Hunting Peoples:*[2]

Boys and girls have no adults to guide them through puberty ordeals that they need in order to maintain social continuity. It is no wonder that they create age-graded micro-societies of their own. The secrecy that once formed a vital part of puberty rites is transferred to their parents, to whom they will not reveal what they have been doing.

A rite of passage or initiation process is an excellent way for adults and youth to come together. Together they can design a series of common activities, rituals, and ceremonies that are appropriate for their own common community needs, traditions and heritage. As a result, they create a powerful and memorable experience in which youth feel and know they are accepted and respected as growing adults.

The model presented here is merely a suggested series of activities, processes, and experiences rather than a specific recipe. The best experiences are created by adult members of a specific community who are passionately involved in the growth of youth and who use their own knowledge of their community's history, heritage, and culture to create a meaningful rite of passage. Parents must be intimately involved and invited to participate.

The model here has been used with schools and other groups that mix boys and girls, including some activities for same-sex groups within that model. Initiation adventures and rituals with total gender separation have been created by The ManKind Project, and Boys to Men Mentoring Network; contact information is listed on page 216.

Basic Concepts

A Community of Safety and Trust

All activities must be conducted within an integrated community of safety and trust. All participants must be honored, and all participants must be accepted for who they are without fear of being put down or ridiculed. When leaders treat youth with respect — that is, avoid "talking down," talking as though they are not present, and talking about them to other adults — youth respond with respect for the adults and for the experience itself.

Safety is established by the demeanor of the adult and youth leadership, by the guidelines and ground rules established, and by movement of activities from low-risk to higher-risk participation. The site itself must be safe, too — free from intrusions once the training has started. A retreat site works best, especially one unknown to the initiates. Facilitators and leaders must constantly read the group, check in with individuals, and confer with each other to make sure everyone is feeling safe.

Entering the Mystery

An atmosphere of expectancy needs to be created, including the all-pervasive attitude that this is an especially serious and important event. An atmosphere of mystery must also be created, including the constant expectation that initiates are stepping into the unknown. If safety has been established, fear of the unknown should not be a problem. Tell the initiates only what you must and keep the activities as secret as possible.

Self-Examination

The rite of passage should encourage the initiates to look at themselves — who they are becoming as men and women, their values and beliefs, their heroes, and their hopes and dreams for the future.

Personal Mission

The initiation should encourage the initiate to develop a sense of mission, including identification of his/her purpose in life and the specific contributions s/he wants to make to society.

The Example of Elders

Youth need to hear from the elders in their community. Invite men and women from as many generations as possible to participate, and ask them to speak openly and honestly from their own life experiences.

Ceremony of Acceptance

Elders need to present symbols of maturity to each initiate as a way of extending a welcome into the adult community. Youth need to bring a symbol of their childhood that they want to give up — an object they are willing to destroy or words on paper that represent an immature part of them that they are willing to change. These symbols are formally exchanged during the ceremony of acceptance.

Celebration

Music, dancing, drumming, humor, and a feast are all essential parts of celebrating youth's passage to adulthood.

Preparation

Site Selection

Select a retreat site where both indoor and outdoor activities are possible without intrusion. Privacy is important for maintaining a sense of mystery and to avoid embarrassment on the part of participants. A camp setting where the group can get away from the normal daily routine is especially good. There needs to be a large room for large group activities. It is also helpful to have two distinctly separate areas for same-sex work.

Lead Facilitators

Select a man and a woman who have experience training youth, a keen sense of what makes an activity appropriate, and a natural ease with youth.

Adult Leaders

Invite a large number of men and women of a variety of ages to work with groups for sections of the retreat and to form the circle of elders. (See Elder Circle on page 148.) Elders are anyone over age twenty-one. For every session, keep a ratio of one adult leader for every ten youth. Select men and women who are good role models, who passionately love youth, who are able to talk with youth with respect and ease, and who are willing and able to participate in all the activities. Parents, grandparents, community workers, teachers, coaches, police officers, firemen, doctors, nurses, and youth ministers are all great.

Youth Leaders

Invite one or two youth leaders for every ten initiates. Youth who have previously been through the experience make excellent leaders. With junior high and middle school groups, try to enlist a senior high boy and girl for each group of eight to ten. They provide role models for the young initiates and bring tremendous energy to the activities.

Planning Team

The two lead facilitators work with the adult and youth leaders to create the experience. Two or three planning meetings should be sufficient.

Symbolic Items

Initiates need to select a childhood item or create on a piece of paper a symbol of something from their childhood. Their willingness to destroy or leave behind this symbol marks their movement into maturity.

Elders need to create or select symbols as gifts to the initiates signifying their acceptance into the adult community. Examples are a sash, cap, bandana, bracelet, necklace, or talisman — anything that would be meaningful within the community.

Questions

Youth and elders need to write down any questions they would like to have answered. (See Question Cards, page 142.)

Materials

In general, you will need flip charts, color markers, tape, pencils and pens, a roll of butcher paper, play dough, index cards, and scissors. After you have planned the activities for your retreat, be sure to check the materials list for each activity for additional supplies that will be needed.

Sample Rite of Passage

Session 1: Building a Safe Community

Welcome and Introductions

Facilitator welcomes group, makes introductions of key people, gives important information (bathrooms, particular rules of the site).

Facilitator explains the general purpose of this event as a special experience designed to initiate and welcome youth into the community of adults: "During this experience we will create a community where it is safe to be yourself. We will examine our life journey so far. We will define what it means to be a man or a woman. We will create ceremonies to celebrate the initiation into adulthood. We will plan service projects to make our community a better place."

Ground Rules

1. **Take care of yourself.**

   Make sure you're having a good time and your needs are met.

2. **Take care of each other.**

   Give each other support and encouragement. Help each other have a good time.

3. **Enter the mystery.**

   Fully participate, jump in, take a risk.

4. **Take care of the space.**

   Make sure everything gets cleaned up. This space should look better when we leave than when we arrived.

Activities

Use team building activities you are familiar with.

The sequence of events needs to begin with low-risk activities — getting to know each other, name games, and large-group activities. Then gradually, as trust grows among the individuals, move toward higher degrees of risk-taking. If done correctly, you will be able to establish among participants the feeling that this is a special and safe place where they can be themselves without fear of being judged or criticized. You want everybody to feel like they will have fun and be okay. Trust and bonding usually moves from trusting the facilitators to trusting the other adult leaders to trusting peers. The outcome should be a feeling of cohesion within the group and a willingness of all initiates to step into the mystery of the experience.

Select activities from Chapter 9, Connecting with Others. Here is a typical activity sequence:

Reach Out and Touch Someone (page 95)

Circle of Life (page 93)

Shapes (page 94)

Body Part Connections (page 104)

Thank You Very Much, But I Gotta Go (page 98)

You Send Me (page 102)

Give Me a Lift (page 108)

Feelings Banners (page 56)

Great Escape (page 106)

See also Michelle Karns, *How to Create Positive Relationships with Students: A Handbook of Group Activities and Teaching Strategies* (Research Press, 1994) and Bob Gregson, *The Incredible Indoor Games Book* (Pitman Learning, 1982).

Session 2: The Journey of Heroes and Dreams

Purpose

Youth identify heroes and the skills and attitudes they represent.

Youth clarify their own values, beliefs, and behaviors.

Youth identify personal dreams, guiding principles, and hopes for the future.

Activities

Select activities that ask youth to identify personal values and beliefs, dreams, guiding principles, mission, and hopes for the future.

Here is a typical activity sequence:

Timelines (page 51)

Cross the Line (page 65)

Heroic Mind Web (page 80)

Hero Tales (page 89)

What Do I Stand For? (page 54)

When Am I in My Power? (page 58)

Life Journey Map (page 70)

Personal Mandala (page 50)

Personal Banners (page 153)

Clay Transformations (page 67)

Session 3: The Journey of Women, The Journey of Men

Purpose

Youth work in same-sex groups to define masculinity, femininity, boundaries, and principles.

Activities

Select activities that lead youth to understand who they are as growing men and women. Here is a typical activity sequence:

Ideas About Men and Women (page 138)

When Am I in My Power? (page 58)

Personal Boundaries (page 152)

How We'd Like to Be Treated (Skit preparation) (page 147)

What Does Respect Look Like? (page 149)

Session 4: The Forum of Women and Men

Purpose

Youth hear from each other and from the council of elders.

Activities

Here is a typical activity sequence:

Fishbowl (page 146)

Question Cards (page 142)

How We'd Like to Be Treated (Skit performance) (page 147)

Elder Circle (page 148)

Session 5: Initiation Ceremony

Purpose

Youth are accepted by elders into the community of adults, giving up a symbol from their childhood and accepting symbols of adulthood.

Activities

During this session, rituals are created to help mark the passage of the initiates from childhood to the adult community. The session revolves around answering some basic questions:

When are you in your power?

When do you feel spiritual?

What is an appropriate symbol for your passage into adulthood?

What symbol of your childhood do you want to leave as you grow into adulthood?

How can the elders in attendance honor and recognize you as you become part of the adult community?

HERE IS A TYPICAL ACTIVITY SEQUENCE leading up to the Initiation Ceremony:

1. When Am I in My Power? (page 58)

2. Clay Transformations (page 67)

3. Youth planning time:

   Ask youth to prepare the objects they have brought to destroy during the initiation ceremony. Ask them as well to create pictures and words depicting concepts, attitudes, and behaviors they would like to leave in their childhood (using paper and markers). Let them decorate these papers and personalize them in their own way. Remind them that these will be destroyed.

4. Elder planning time:

   Ask elders to prepare the symbols they plan to present to the youth during the initiation ceremony. Ask them to select appropriate music, words, actions, or symbols to use in the following ceremony. Most of the initiation ceremony needs to be secret, as the youth need to "step into the mystery" of the ceremony.

Initiation Ceremony

The best initiation ceremonies are designed by the council of elders and are held at night. Both elders and youth must be encouraged to take the ceremony seriously while acting joyfully.

Sample Initiation Ceremony

Take initiates to a separate room. Blindfold each initiate before leaving the room.

Carefully lead each initiate to the ceremonial space.

Elders stand in a circle, drumming and making noise with noise-makers.

Outside the circle, each initiate is asked this question:
  "You are invited to join the community of men and women. Will you accept the rights and the responsibilities of becoming an adult?"

Remove blindfold. Lead initiate to center of circle.

Ask the initiate to hand over (or burn in the fire) the object or paper that represents part of his/her youth s/he is willing to give over.

Give to the initiate the chosen symbols of adulthood.

Introduce the initiate to the community of adults (some youth elect to create a ceremonial or adult name).

The community applauds and the initiate joins the circle of adults.

After all initiates have come into the circle, there is drumming and celebration, and the initiates are led to a feast in their honor.

If the experiences leading up to the ceremony have been genuine and authentic, then the ceremony will be genuine and authentic as well. The best and most meaningful ceremonies include the initiates' significant adults in both the design and implementation of the ceremony, and they also honor the heritage and traditions of the community.

Session 6: The Journey of Deeds

Purpose

Youth and adults create realistic plans for stewardship and service that reflect their personal values and missions.

Activities

Create a sequence of activities resulting in a choice of bold, meaningful, achievable tasks that allow youth to make a difference in their school or community. The activities here are framed for use in an educational environment, but they can easily be reframed for community use with a few simple word changes in the directions.

HERE IS A TYPICAL ACTIVITY SEQUENCE:

Card Castles (page 158)

Build Me a World (page 159)

Ideal School (or Community) (page 160)

Keep, Change, and Build (page 162)

Action Planning (page 163)

Many youth complain that they spend a lot of time planning and seldom get to see their plans manifest into reality. Encourage the adult leaders to support the action plans by continuing to have follow-up sessions with youth as a way of ensuring they accomplish the planned deeds.

Session 7: Closure

Purpose

To bring the experience to a close.

Activity

Peace Quilt (page 165)

Group sits in a large circle.

Ask each person to read his/her peace quilt contribution.

Ask each person to relate a comment about the experience.

Facilitator ends experience.

Character Education in Schools: The Resiliency, Youth Development, Asset-Building Continuum

Over the last two decades, we have been working with schools in many districts and at all levels to apply the latest research findings in character education. As we interacted with teachers, curriculum designers, administrators, and counselors, we have been able to apply this research in practical ways to create learning experiences that can be integrated into the existing school program. Our goals were to enhance the general curriculum and to help children develop the skills, knowledge, aptitudes, and practices they need to grow up to be healthy and responsible adults. In this appendix, we will summarize the main points of the character education research and how this research can be applied to school-based programs.

Three compelling research-based approaches to character education for youth have emerged over the past three decades. The first approach centers on developing *Resiliency*; the second, *Youth Development,* focuses on fostering specific skills youth need to live healthy lives; and the third, *Asset Building,* identifies 40 basic developmental assets in eight areas that youth need during their formative years.

Resiliency

Resiliency researchers looked for traits and characteristics of children coming out of situations of adversity and tragedy who adapted successfully. The concept of resiliency has been applied to all children:

> The evolution of the definition of resiliency to an ability to spring back, rebound, and/or successfully adapt in the face of adversity including all the environmental risks, personal traumas and tragedies, or emotional disabili-

ties, clarifies why every young person alive (indeed, every person of any age!) needs to develop resiliency. (Henderson, 1997, p. 23)

Resilient youth exhibit high self-esteem, believe in their own efficacy, possess a repertoire of solution-finding skills, have the ability to analyze situations critically, and think creatively. They tend to be achievement oriented, socially connected, and future focused. They are sensitive to personal boundaries, open to help when needed, and careful to withdraw from negative situations.

Schools and classrooms that produce resilient youth have the following characteristics: caring relationships, high expectations, and opportunities to participate (Benard, 1997). In fact, the concept of resiliency and its development is predicated on the quality of relationships among children and the influential adults in their lives.

The resiliency researchers encourage schools to create activities in the following areas (Henderson & Milstein, 1996):

1. Provide opportunities for meaningful participation.

   Students are viewed as workers, teachers as coaches.

   Everyone's contribution is viewed as important.

   Members grow and learn by sharing and treating each other with respect.

   Potentially positive new experiences are encouraged.

2. Increase prosocial bonding.

   Positive and supportive organizational climate and culture exists.

   Equity, reasonable risk-tasking, and learning are promoted.

   Visions and missions are clearly communicated and agreed upon.

3. Set clear, consistent boundaries.

   Cooperation and support exist.

   Schoolwide objectives are shared.

   Members are involved in setting policies and rules.

4. Teach "life skills."

   Efforts are made to improve the school.

   Sensible risk-taking is supported, as are individual and group skill development.

   Positive role modeling is practiced.

5. Provide caring and support.

   Members have a sense of belonging.

   Cooperation is encouraged.

   Celebrations of success are practiced.

Leaders spend lots of positive time with members.

Resources are obtained with a minimum of effort.

6. Set and communicate high expectations.

Individual efforts are viewed as important.

Reasonable risk-taking is promoted.

"Can do!" attitudes prevail.

Individualized growth plans are developed and monitored.

The resiliency approach, with its emphasis on caring and empowering relationships, seeks to support vulnerable youth with both one-to-one and in-group activities in the moment and in the classroom.

Youth Development

Youth development can best be defined as an ongoing process that engages all youth in meeting their basic personal and social needs as they mature as well as building the competencies necessary for a successful adolescence and adult life. The youth development process focuses on youth's strengths, capacities, and developmental requirements with less emphasis on their weaknesses and problems. The premise is that in order to succeed as adults, all youth must acquire positive attitudes and appropriate behaviors and skills in six areas: health, personal/social, knowledge, reasoning and creativity, vocation, and citizenship (Politz, 1996).

Through a structured, progressive series of activities and experiences in these six skill areas, the youth development process focuses on the broader developmental assets that children and youth need, such as caring relationships, safe places and activities, physical and mental health, marketable skills, and opportunities for service and civic participation (National Collaboration for Youth, 2000). Youth are helped to become competent socially, morally, emotionally, physically, and cognitively.

Asset Building

Extending the resiliency and youth development approaches, Dr. Peter Benson and the Search Institute have identified 20 external and 20 internal assets (see the chart on the following page). These assets are "positive experiences and qualities – 'developmental assets' – that have tremendous influence on young people's lives" (Benson, 1997, p. 19). The asset-building approach is in essence a philosophy and it includes anyone touching the lives of youth. Families, schools, neighborhoods, congregations, and all organizations, institu-

The Search Institute 40 Developmental Assets

CATEGORY	ASSET NAME AND DEFINITION

<table>
<tr><td rowspan="20">EXTERNAL ASSETS</td></tr>
</table>

Support

1. **Family support**—Family life provides high levels of love and support.
2. **Positive family communication**—Young person and her or his parent(s) communicate positively, and young person is willing to seek advice and counsel from parent(s).
3. **Other adult relationships**—Young person receives support from three or more nonparent adults.
4. **Caring neighborhood**—Young person experiences caring neighbors.
5. **Caring school climate**—School provides a caring, encouraging environment.
6. **Parent involvement in schooling**—Parent(s) are actively involved in helping young person succeed in school.

Empowerment

7. **Community values youth**—Young person perceives that adults in the community value youth.
8. **Youth as resources**—Young people are given useful roles in the community.
9. **Service to others**—Young person serves in the community one hour or more per week.
10. **Safety**—Young person feels safe at home, at school, and in the neighborhood.

Boundaries and Expectations

11. **Family boundaries**—Family has clear rules and consequences and monitors the young person's whereabouts.
12. **School boundaries**—School provides clear rules and consequences.
13. **Neighborhood boundaries**—Neighbors take responsibility for monitoring young people's behavior.
14. **Adult role models**—Parent(s) and other adults model positive, responsible behavior.
15. **Positive peer influence**—Young person's best friends model responsible behavior.
16. **High expectations**—Both parent(s) and teachers encourage the young person to do well.

Constructive Use of Time

17. **Creative activities**—Young person spends three or more hours per week in lessons or practice in music, theater, or other arts.
18. **Youth programs**—Young person spends three or more hours per week in sports, clubs, or organizations at school and/or in the community.
19. **Religious community**—Young person spends one or more hours per week in activities in a religious institution.
20. **Time at home**—Young person is out with friends "with nothing special to do" two or fewer nights per week.

INTERNAL ASSETS

Commitment to Learning

21. **Achievement motivation**—Young person is motivated to do well in school.
22. **School engagement**—Young person is actively engaged in learning.
23. **Homework**—Young person reports doing at least one hour of homework every school day.
24. **Bonding to school**—Young person cares about her or his school.
25. **Reading for pleasure**—Young person reads for pleasure three or more hours per week.

Positive Values

26. **Caring**—Young person places high value on helping other people.
27. **Equality and social justice**—Young person places high value on promoting equality and reducing hunger and poverty.
28. **Integrity**—Young person acts on convictions and stands up for her or his beliefs.
29. **Honesty**—Young person "tells the truth even when it is not easy."
30. **Responsibility**—Young person accepts and takes personal responsibility.
31. **Restraint**—Young person believes it is important not to be sexually active or to use alcohol or other drugs.

Social Competencies

32. **Planning and decision making**—Young person knows how to plan ahead and make choices.
33. **Interpersonal competence**—Young person has empathy, sensitivity, and friendship skills.
34. **Cultural competence**—Young person has knowledge of and comfort with people of different cultural/racial/ethnic backgrounds.
35. **Resistance skills**—Young person can resist negative peer pressure and dangerous situations.
36. **Peaceful conflict resolution**—Young person seeks to resolve conflict nonviolently.

Positive Identity

37. **Personal power**—Young person feels he or she has control over "things that happen to me."
38. **Self-esteem**—Young person reports having a high self-esteem.
39. **Sense of purpose**—Young person reports that "my life has a purpose."
40. **Positive view of personal future**—Young person is optimistic about her or his personal future.

tions, and individuals in a community can play a role in building assets in youth.

In *The Troubled Journey*, Peter Benson challenges educators to:

- Personalize schools so that each and every child feels cared for, supported, and important.

- Enhance social competencies, including friendship-making skills, caring skills, assertiveness skills, and resistance skills.

- Emphasize the development of positive values, particularly those that build a sense of personal responsibility for the welfare of others.

- Offer quality prevention programming in multiple areas of risk-taking including alcohol, tobacco, illicit drugs, suicide and depression, sexuality, and vehicle safety.

- Enhance academic effectiveness to ensure that students in all income levels gain in academic motivation and competence.

- Emphasize service learning programs, seeking to provide all students with helping opportunities and personal reflections on the meaning of helping.

- Provide strong support services for youth at risk. (Benson, 1993, p. 81)

The Search Institute research indicates that when youth have few of these assets, their vulnerability to alcohol abuse, sexual activity, violent and antisocial behaviors increases. This vulnerability dramatically decreases as the number of assets increases. Additionally, positive behaviors, such as success in school, personal health, etc., increase as new assets are acquired. According to the Search Institute research, the average sixth to twelfth grader has about 18 of the 40 assets. Only 8 percent of young people ever acquire as many as 31 to 40 assets (Roehlkepartain, 1999).

The strength of the asset-building approach is its delineation of 40 specific assets that can be fostered in a variety of settings. Its community-based emphasis seeks to unite home, school, and community with a positive vision of youth by creating a culture that values the young on their journey to adulthood.

The implementation of the asset-building approach has been greatly enhanced by the work of Russell Quaglia and his colleagues at the National Center for Student Aspirations at the University of Maine's Department of Education. This group has identified eight asset-building conditions that teachers can rely on to promote student aspirations directly in the classroom (Quaglia & Fox, 1998):

1. Belonging: Students being valued members of a community while maintaining their individuality

2. Sense of Accomplishment: Students being recognized for their academic,

social, and personal growth

3. Heroes: Students being comfortable with someone in their lives they can turn to for advice, support, and encouragement

4. Fun and Excitement: Students being engaged and exhibiting genuine enjoyment and endless energy toward activities

5. Curiosity and Creativity: Students being pioneers in exploring "why" and "why not"

6. Spirit of Adventure: Students being confident and prepared to meet new challenges

7. Leadership and Responsibility: Students being able to express their ideas and willing to accept the consequences of their actions

8. Confidence to Take Action: Students being able to set high goals and willing to put forth the necessary effort to achieve them

Quaglia (Quaglia & Fox, 1998) defines students aspirations as "an individual's ability to identify and set goals for the future, while being inspired in the present to work toward those goals." This definition is based on his research which found that many students have a discordance between their aspirations and their motivation, with students describing their aspirations as:

I want to be a doctor, but I don't like science.
I want to be a community leader, but I don't like too much responsibility.
I want to go to college, but I don't like to study.

The eight asset-building conditions that Quaglia identified are arranged to lead students not only to construct hopes and dreams but also to generate the motivation and discipline to achieve them. In this way, action becomes coherent with their desires and dreams. Quaglia (Quaglia & Fox, 1998) arranges the conditions hierarchically in three clusters:

1. Foundations for Aspirations: Belonging, Heroes, Sense of Accomplishment

2. Motivation and Enthusiasm for Aspirations: Fun and Excitement, Spirit of Adventure, Curiosity and Creativity

3. Lifelong Aspirations Mindset: Leadership and Responsibility, Confidence to Take Action

This common-sense approach allows teachers to integrate asset- and aspiration-building directly into the curriculum.

How *Reviving the Wonder* Relates to Character Education in Schools

In designing the activities in *Reviving the Wonder*, we have integrated the asset-building approach toward developing resilient youth with the aspirations model, focusing on what teachers can apply in the classroom. Part One, Optimum Learning Environments, was inspired by the eight conditions Quaglia describes and focuses on five conditions for asset building and resiliency promotion: hope, humor, heroes, head, and heart.

In Part Two, The Personal Journey, and Part Three, Transformations, we gleaned from the 40 assets those that could be specifically and directly affected by classroom teachers. The activities in Parts Two and Three are directly correlated to the eight categories of assets and they promote 20 of the 40 assets.

Teachers, counselors, and other educators interested in direct and positive character education programming can organize these activities into thematic teaching units. Appendix Two elaborates on how schools have integrated *Reviving the Wonder* into their curricula and presents activity sequences and ways of organizing the activities as teaching units.

References

Benard, B. (1997). Resiliency research: A foundation for youth development. *Resiliency in Action,* Winter, 13-18.

Benson, P.L. (1993). *The troubled journey.* Minneapolis, MN: Search Institute.

Benson, P.L. (1997). Connecting resiliency, youth development, and asset development in a positive-focused framework for youth. *Resiliency in Action,* Winter, 19-22.

Henderson, N. (1997). Resiliency and asset development: A continuum for youth success. *Resiliency in Action,* Winter, 23-27.

Henderson, N., & Milstein, M. (1996). *Resiliency in school: Making it happen for students and educators.* Thousand Oaks, CA: Corwin Press.

National Collaboration for Youth (2000). *Younger Americans Act Policy Proposal, April 7, 2000.* Washington, DC: Author.

Politz, B. (1996). *Making the case: Community foundations and youth development* (2nd ed.). Washington, DC: Center for Youth Development and Policy Research, Foundations for Change.

Quaglia, R.J., & Fox, K.M. (1998). *Believing in achieving.* Orono, ME: National Center for Student Aspirations.

Roehlkepartain, E.C. (1999). *You can make a difference for kids.* Minneapolis, MN: 3M Corporation and Search Institute.

Using *Reviving the Wonder* in the School Curriculum

S everal schools that we consult with have used the activities in *Reviving the Wonder* throughout the school year as part of their regular curriculum. Some schools integrate the activities into the academic curriculum while other schools use the activities on their own. This appendix presents two examples of teaching formats: (1) a 12-week interdisciplinary approach in which the activities are integrated with the academic subjects and (2) a 9-week classroom-based approach in which the classroom teacher facilitates the activities without integrating them with other disciplines in the academic curriculum. Each teaching format presents theme-based units, which have daily lesson/activity plans. Each unit states the purpose, the activity sequence for each week, outcomes, evaluation, and how the unit relates to the character education approaches that focus on asset building, aspirations, and resiliency. (See Appendix One for a discussion of these character education approaches.) Both formats rely on the use of journals, quiet time, and reflection groups.

> **Journals.** We recommend that students keep a journal for recording their personal reflections, ideas, notes, thoughts, and sketches. The journal will then become the basis for personal essays, ideas for group discussion, and notes about projects. Students should make their own journals, rather than purchasing them. We have found that when students construct and personalize their own journals, their work is more thoughtful and expansive.
>
> **Quiet Time.** Students need time for personal reflection, time to think, dream, and create. We recommend that teachers build one or two 20-minute periods into the schedule each week so that students can work with their journals.
>
> **Reflection Groups.** As part of the small-group experience, we recommend that students share self-selected parts of their journals with the group. One of the 20-minute periods mentioned above can be used for this purpose.

Format 1
A 12-Week Interdisciplinary Approach

This format organizes the activities into six units taught over the course of 12 weeks and integrates the activities with the academic subject areas.

The Elements of an Interdisciplinary Approach

Literature Unit

The activities provide an excellent basis for literature units. For example, the activities in "Part Two: The Personal Journey" can be used to examine literature related to issues involved in growing up. Appropriate resources include the classics, such as Shakespeare's *Hamlet* and *Romeo and Juliet*, James Joyce's *A Portrait of the Artist as a Young Man*, Anne Frank's *Diary of a Young Girl* as well as contemporary writers, such as S.E. Hinton's books *The Outsiders* and *Tex*.

Depending on the age and reading level of the class, teachers can compile a varied and fascinating collection of titles from which young readers can choose. There also are a number of films available on videotape that feature the trials of growing up. The film *Good Will Hunting*, for example, is an excellent portrayal of youth-mentor relationships. Consult with a librarian specializing in children and young adult literature to select relevant books and other media.

We recommend selecting one or two titles for the entire class to study as a corollary to their own experiences and as an impetus to their own writing and sketches in their journals. Class activities can include:

- Book/videotape discussions – Classroom discourse on the impact that a book or videotape had on the students

- Book reports – The traditional book-report essay approach, but with special emphasis on the protagonist's struggle with growing up

- Dramatized selections of meaningful parts of the selected works

- Videotaped book reports and dramatizations

- Student panel presentations to class followed by a question-and-answer period

We recommend devoting one day per week to literature activities with new books and new writing projects assigned in 6-week cycles.

Writing Lab

In addition to the students writing in their journals, one class per week can be used as a writing lab in which students can work on longer term writing assignments. They can work on individual projects, obtain advice from the teacher, and share "works in progress" with other students. Student writing projects can include:

- Poetry based on the students' personal experiences

- Short stories, character sketches, and reflections based on the students' lives, with the real-life events used as the basis for fictionalized accounts

- Photo essays based on students' personal experiences including photos and writing on such topics as mentors, family members and family history, and persons or organizations that have made a positive difference in the lives of others

- Reflective essays on selected poems and stories by published authors

- Autobiographies discussing personal missions, goals, aspirations, and future plans

- Biographies of family and neighborhood or community heroes

- Biographies of inspirational historical figures

- Essays on how various cultures initiate and integrate their youth

- Collections of newspaper clippings about people making a positive difference in the community accompanied by interviews with these people conducted by the students

Field Trips

Field trips such as the following can enrich the students' experience:

- Trips to the locales of historical heroes

- Visits to local citizens who are making a difference in the community

- Visits to organizations offering service to people in the community

- A Ropes Course experience

Guest Speakers

Guest speakers can provide students with a wealth of information about their communities and about handling the issues that students face as they grow up. Speakers can include:

- People in the community who are making a positive difference, particularly those performing community service and community leadership

- A panel of similar speakers, such as a group of grandparents, to talk about their experiences growing up and to share the wisdom of their years

- Police and fire personnel, directors of human service agencies, elected officials, and representatives from service clubs such as the Optimists, Lions, Elks, or Rotary

Homework Assignments

Homework assignments can be made to continue the theme of the activities, such as writing and sketching in journals, reading assignments, mentor/hero interviews, and long-term writing projects.

Discipline Inclusion

Reviving the Wonder activities can be integrated across disciplines with a team of teachers from different disciplines using one or more of the activities in coordination with each other's classes.

Literature. Teachers can create a corollary literature unit with reflective activities that match the themes of each unit.

Creative Writing. Teachers can use writing lab assignments in their classes, such as character sketches, poetry, short stories, and scripts, for dramatic presentations by the students and for videotape presentations.

Nonfiction Writing. Writing lab options can be expanded by including photo essays, interview reports, biographies of mentors, autobiographies, and book reports.

Research Writing. Research reports can be based on biographies of heroic lives or interviews with community leaders.

Art. Art activities can include book-making, portraits and self-portraits, photo essays, sculpture, symbol-making, and reflective art interpretations.

Social Studies. Teachers can request reports about how different cultures initiate youth into adult society.

Preparing for the 12-Week Interdisciplinary Approach

These "get ready" suggestions will help the 12-week sequence run smoothly.

- Create a book-making area in the classroom where students can find cardboard, paper, cloth, glue, scissors, and brass tabs to use for making their journals. Or, create a materials list and directions so that students can assemble their own materials to bring in for making their journals (see Homemade Books, page 40).

- Identify and contact guest speakers and schedule specific dates and times for their presentations.

- Consult a librarian and/or media specialist about an appropriate selection of books and videotapes. The subject areas will include issues about growing up, biographies and autobiographies of heroic men and women, and descriptions of how other cultures initiate youth into adult society.

- Plan a sequence of activities if you select one book for all student to read.

- Select and create instructions for writing projects.

- Identify locations for field trips and make transportation arrangements.

- Coordinate your teaching schedule with other teachers who will be integrating the activities in their subject-area classes.

Establishing a Basic Weekly Teaching Schedule

Many teachers use a standard weekly schedule after the *Reviving the Wonder* activities are under way. This schedule is based on traditional class periods. Block scheduling allows for greater time flexibility and more imaginative sequencing. The following is an example of a basic weekly teaching schedule.

Monday. *Reviving the Wonder* activity: Select an appropriate activity or sequence of activities. Be sure to close the activity by "debriefing" the students about the content of the activity.

Tuesday. Literature activities: Use chapter discussion, reflection activities, book reports, dramatization, panel discussions, or simply silent reading.

Wednesday. *Reviving the Wonder* activity.

Thursday. Writing lab: Work on long-term writing assignment or share "works in progress."

Friday. You may conduct a *Reviving the Wonder* activity or make Fridays unique by having small-group reflections, journal work or discussions, guest speakers, field trips, or showing videotapes.

Unit 1 Creating a Classroom Community

Purpose

To transform the class from a collection of individuals into a community of learners

To engage the students in the learning components

To promote bonding among students by helping them discover their differences while honoring their similarities

To set ground rules needed to complete the work of the learning experience

To create a process for conflict resolution

To introduce the themes and concepts of the learning experience

To develop a vision for the learning experience

To promote a positive work ethic among the students

To inaugurate the literature program and writing lab projects

Week 1 Activity Sequence

Monday	Tuesday	Wednesday	Thursday	Friday
Introduce the unit and discuss the overall purpose and themes. Choose from the following activities: • Circle of Life (page 93) • Thank You Very Much, But I Gotta Go (page 98) • Circles and Circles (page 99)	Create a positive work ethic and code of ethics for the learning experience. Choose from the following activities: • Three Crucial Rules (page 9) • Integrity (page 69)	Choose from the following bonding activities: • Sweet Talk (page 48) • Mingle, Mingle (page 100) • You Send Me (page 102) • Body Part Connections (page 104)	Journal making: • Homemade Books (page 40)	Journal making (continued) and discussion of using the journal: • Homemade Books (page 40)

Week 2 Activity Sequence

Monday	Tuesday	Wednesday	Thursday	Friday
Choose from the following bonding activities: • Aces and Faces (page 105) • Card Castles (page 158)	Literature activities and writing lab activities, including book selection and writing project selection	Choose from the following trust-building activities: • Circle of Support (page 107) • Give Me a Lift (page 108)	Conflict resolution: • Clearing a Conflict (page 110)	Reflections group, journal work, field trip, guest speaker, or videotape

Outcomes

Students will feel that they are part of a community.

Students will understand the basic practices, including rights and rules, work ethic, and conflict resolution.

Students will create and use a journal.

Students will select a book for study.

Students will decide on a writing project.

Evaluation

Evaluations can be based on the construction quality of the journals and participation in group activities and discussions.

Character Education Approaches

Asset-Building Focus			Aspirations Focus	Resiliency Focus
5. Caring school climate	28. Integrity		Belonging	Increase prosocial bonding
10. Safety	29. Honesty		Fun and excitement	Set clear, consistent boundaries
12. School boundaries	30. Responsibility			Provide caring and support
15. Positive peer influence	33. Interpersonal competence			
16. High expectations	34. Cultural competence			
22. School engagement	36. Peaceful conflict resolution			
24. Bonding to school				

191

Unit 2 The Inner Me

Purpose

To examine values, beliefs, personal principles, and talents

To create a language for describing feelings

To identify personal aspirations and contributions

To compare their outer public image to their interior personality

Week 3 Activity Sequence

Monday	Tuesday	Wednesday	Thursday	Friday
Choose from the following activities: • Paper People (page 49) • Personal Mandala (page 50)	Literature activities that include novels, short stories, poems, films, plays, and essays that focus on the issues of growing up	• Timelines (page 51)	Writing lab activities that focus on personal explorations in the form of poems, sketches, stories, or essays	Reflections group, journal work, field trip, guest speaker, or videotape. If you wish to conduct an activity, use: • What Do I Stand For? (page 54)

Week 4 Activity Sequence

Monday	Tuesday	Wednesday	Thursday	Friday
• Feelings Banners (page 56)	Literature activities or continue with the Feelings Banners activity	• When Am I in My Power? (page 58)	Writing lab or literature activities	Reflections group, journal work, field trip, guest speaker, or videotape

Week 5 Activity Sequence

Monday	Tuesday	Wednesday	Thursday	Friday
• Grab Bag (page 55)	Literature activities	Choose from the following activities: • Tri-Fold (page 63) • Life Journey Map (page 70) • The Mask I Wear (page 71)	Choose from the three activities listed for Wednesday and/or continue with one of these activities.	Reflections group, journal work, field trip, guest speaker, or videotape. If you wish to conduct an activity, choose from the three activities listed for Wednesday.

Week 6 Activity Sequence

Monday	Tuesday	Wednesday	Thursday	Friday
• Personal Brochure (page 60)	Literature activity	Continue with the Personal Brochure activity.	Writing lab activities	Reflections group, journal work, field trip, guest speaker, or videotape

Outcomes

Students will increase their understanding of personal goals, aspirations, talents, values, and feelings.

Students will be able to discuss and express their feelings more easily.

Students will develop personal brochures describing themselves.

Evaluation

Evaluations can be based on the quality of the personal brochures, journal entries, participation in group activities and discussions, quiz results for the reading activities, and the writing projects.

Character Education Approaches

Asset-Building Focus	Aspirations Focus	Resiliency Focus
37. Personal power	Sense of accomplishment	Set and communicate high expectations
38. Self-esteem	Curiosity and creativity	
39. Sense of purpose	Spirit of adventure	
40. Positive view of personal future		

Unit 3 Heroes, Role Models, and Mentors

Purpose

To identify role models and mentors in everyday life

To identify and emulate positive role models in the community

To identify admirable historical heroes

To rectify any personal characteristics that do not contribute to being a future positive role model

Week 7 Activity Sequence

Monday	Tuesday	Wednesday	Thursday	Friday
• Heroic Quotations (page 77)	Literature activities with emphasis on biographies and autobiographies of heroic lives	• Heroes: Think, Feel, Act (page 81)	Writing lab activities that focus on biographies of role models, interviews of outstanding community leaders, or researched essays on heroic lives	Reflections group, journal work, field trip, guest speaker, or videotape. If you wish to conduct an activity, choose from: • Animal Heroes (page 85) • Sticky Paper Heroes (page 86)

Week 8 Activity Sequence

Monday	Tuesday	Wednesday	Thursday	Friday
• Support Chart (page 87)	Literature activity	Introduce the following activity and have students prepare for the activity: • Generation Interviews (page 88)	Writing lab	Discuss the Generation Interviews activity and have reflections group, journal work, field trip, guest speaker, or videotape

Week 9 Activity Sequence (Monday and Tuesday)

Monday	Tuesday	Wednesday	Thursday	Friday
• Elder Circle (page 148)	Literature activities			

Week 9 completes Unit 3 on Tuesday and begins Unit 4 on Wednesday.

Outcomes

Students will identify personal role models.

Students will create biographies of their role models

Students will research the lives of their heroes.

Students will identify personal characteristics they want to emulate.

Evaluation

Evaluations can be based on the quality of journal work; writing projects on role models and heroes; literature activities, quizzes, and tests; and participation in group activities and discussions.

Character Education Approaches

Asset-Building Focus	Aspirations Focus	Resiliency Focus
3. Other adult relationships	Heroes	Teach "life skills"
14. Adult role models	Leadership and responsibility	
26. Caring		
28. Integrity		
29. Honesty		
30. Responsibility		

Unit 4 Personal Mission

Purpose

To construct personal mission statements that examine values, principles, characteristics, talents, aspirations, and contributions

Week 9 Activity Sequence (Wednesday, Thursday, Friday)

Monday	Tuesday	Wednesday	Thursday	Friday
		• Personal Dreams (page 124)	Choose from the following activities:	Reflections group, journal work, field trip, guest speaker, or videotape. If you wish to conduct an activity, use:
			• What I Value in Life (page 125)	• Personal Mission Statement (page 133)
			• Characteristics I Admire (page 127)	
			• Strengths versus Roadblocks (page 129)	
			• Contributions I Hope to Make (page 131)	

Week 9 completes Unit 3 on Tuesday and begins Unit 4 on Wednesday.

Outcome

Each student will create a clear and concise personal mission statement.

Evaluation

Evaluations can be based on the quality of the written mission statements.

Character Education Approaches

Asset-Building Focus	Aspirations Focus	Resiliency Focus
16. High expectations	Leadership and responsibility	Set and communicate high expectations
26. Caring	Confidence to take action	
28. Integrity		
29. Honesty		
30. Responsibility		
32. Planning and decision making		
37. Personal power		
38. Self-esteem		
39. Sense of purpose		
40. Positive view of personal future		

Unit 5 Gender Definition and Boundaries

Purpose

To identify the unique characteristics of boys and girls

To identify their own unique characteristics as growing men and women

To define appropriate and respectful boundaries between the sexes

To listen to the personal concerns of the opposite sex

Week 10 Activity Sequence

Monday	Tuesday	Wednesday	Thursday	Friday
Choose from the following activities: • Ideas About Men and Women (page 138) • Separate Tables (page 150)	Literature activities that focus on gender definition and boundaries	• Media Images (page 139)	Writing lab activities that focus on gender definition and boundaries	Reflections group, journal work, field trip, guest speaker, or videotape. If you wish to conduct an activity, use: • Personal Banners (page 153)

Week 11 Activity Sequence

Monday	Tuesday	Wednesday	Thursday	Friday
• Situation Cards (page 144)	• How We'd Like to Be Treated (page 147)	• Fishbowl (page 146)	• What Does Respect Look Like? (page 149)	Reflections group, journal work, field trip, guest speaker, or videotape. If you wish to conduct an activity, use: • Personal Attachments (page 109)

Outcomes

Students will understand the unique differences and positive attributes of each sex.

Students will create a cogent code of ethics and boundary definition for how the sexes should treat each other.

Students will understand how the opposite sex wants to be treated.

Evaluation

Evaluations can be based on the quality of literature activities and writing projects as well as participation in the interactive activities.

Character Education Approaches

Asset-Building Focus	Aspirations Focus	Resiliency Focus
26. Caring	Spirit of adventure	Increase prosocial bonding
27. Equality and social justice	Leadership and responsibility	Set clear, consistent boundaries
33. Interpersonal competence		
34. Cultural competence		
35. Resistance skills		
37. Personal power		

Unit 6 Stewardship

Purpose

To evaluate the need for services within the school community

To create effective action plans to meet the unmet needs in the school community

To perform acts of service and stewardship

Week 12 Activity Sequence

Monday	Tuesday	Wednesday	Thursday	Friday
Choose from the following activities: • Card Castles (page 158) • Build Me a World (page 159)	• Ideal School (page 160)	• Keep, Change, and Build (page 162)	• Action Planning (page 163)	• Peace Quilt (page 165)

Outcome

Students will create a bold and doable action plan for acts of stewardship in the school community.

Evaluation

Evaluations can be based on the quality and practicality of the action plan.

Character Education Approaches

Asset-Building Focus	Aspirations Focus	Resiliency Focus
7. Community values youth 8. Youth as resources 9. Service to others 32. Planning and decision making 39. Sense of purpose	Leadership and responsibility Confidence to take action	Provide opportunities for meaningful participation

Optional Culminating Activities

A Literature and Writing Event

Create a performance event in which students present dramatizations from their readings, share excerpts from their writing projects, or show relevant drawings and art objects.

Rite of Passage

Create a rite of passage event by and for students and parents. This event should include a ceremony in which students give up a symbol of their childhood and accept a symbol of their entry into adulthood from their parents. This event should include a letter from all parents detailing their support of their children and their approval of their children's personal mission statements (see Rites of Passage and Initiation, pages 167–175).

Format 2
A 9-Week Classroom-Based Approach

This format is ideal for classroom use when teachers want to use the activities on their own without integrating them with the academic subject areas. It organizes the activities into six units taught over the course of 9 weeks.

Unit 1 Creating a Classroom Community

Purpose

To transform the class from a collection of individuals into a community of learners

To engage the students in the learning components

To promote bonding among students by helping them discover their differences while honoring their similarities

To set ground rules needed to complete the work of the learning experience

To create a process for conflict resolution

To introduce the themes and concepts of the learning experience

To develop a vision for the learning experience

To promote a positive work ethic among the students

To inaugurate the literature program and writing lab projects

Week 1 Activity Sequence

Monday

Introduce the unit and discuss the overall purpose and themes. Choose from the following activities:

- Circle of Life (page 93)
- Thank You Very Much, But I Gotta Go (page 98)
- Circles and Circles (page 99)

Tuesday

Create a positive work ethic and code of ethics for the learning experience. Choose from the following activities:

- Three Crucial Rules (page 9)
- Integrity (page 69)

Wednesday

Choose from the following bonding activities:

- Sweet Talk (page 48)
- Mingle, Mingle (page 100)
- You Send Me (page 102)
- Body Part Connections (page 104)

Thursday

Journal making:

- Homemade Books (page 40)

Friday

Journal making (continued) and discussion of using the journal:

- Homemade Books (page 40)

Week 2 Activity Sequence

Monday

- Aces and Faces (page 105)

Tuesday

- Card Castles (page 158)

Wednesday

Choose from the following trust-building activities:

- Circle of Support (page 107)
- Give Me a Lift (page 108)

Thursday

Conflict resolution:

- Clearing a Conflict (page 110)

Friday

Reflections group, journal work, field trip, guest speaker, or videotape

Outcomes and Evaluation See page 191.   **Character Education Approaches: Asset-Building Focus, Aspirations Focus, Resiliency Focus** See page 191.

Unit 2 The Inner Me

Purpose

To examine values, beliefs, personal principles, and talents

To create a language for describing feelings

To identify personal aspirations and contributions

To compare their outer public image to their interior personality

Week 3 Activity Sequence

Monday	Tuesday	Wednesday	Thursday	Friday
Choose from the following activities: • Paper People (page 49) • Personal Mandala (page 50)	• Timelines (page 51)	• Feelings Banners (page 56)	• When Am I in My Power? (page 58)	Reflections group, journal work, field trip, guest speaker, or videotape

Week 4 Activity Sequence

Monday	Tuesday	Wednesday	Thursday	Friday
• Grab Bag (page 55)	Choose from the following activities: • Tri-Fold (page 63) • Life Journey Map (page 70) • The Mask I Wear (page 71)	Choose from the three activities listed for Tuesday and/or continue with one of these activities.	Choose from the three activities listed for Tuesday and/or continue with one of these activities.	• Personal Brochure (page 60)

Outcomes and Evaluation See page 193.　　**Character Education Approaches: Asset-Building Focus, Aspirations Focus, Resiliency Focus** See page 193.

Unit 3 Heroes, Role Models, and Mentors

Purpose

To identify role models and mentors in everyday life

To identify and emulate positive role models in the community

To identify admirable historical heroes

To rectify any personal characteristics that do not contribute to being a future positive role model

Week 5 Activity Sequence

Monday	Tuesday	Wednesday	Thursday	Friday
• Heroic Quotations (page 77)	• Heroes: Think, Feel, Act (page 81)	Choose from the following activities: • Animal Heroes (page 85) • Sticky Paper Heroes (page 86)	• Support Chart (page 87)	Reflections group, journal work, field trip, guest speaker, or videotape

Week 6 Activity Sequence (Monday and Tuesday)

Monday	Tuesday	Wednesday	Thursday	Friday
• Generation Interviews (page 88)	• Elder Circle (page 148)	Week 6 completes Unit 3 on Tuesday and begins Unit 4 on Wednesday.		

Outcomes and Evaluation See page 195.   **Character Education Approaches: Asset-Building Focus, Aspirations Focus, Resiliency Focus** See page 195.

Unit 4 Personal Mission

Purpose

To construct personal mission statements that examine values, principles, characteristics, talents, aspirations, and contributions

Week 6 Activity Sequence (Wednesday, Thursday, Friday)

Monday	Tuesday	Wednesday	Thursday	Friday
		• Personal Dreams (page 124)	Choose from the following activities: • What I Value in Life (page 125) • Characteristics I Admire (page 127) • Strengths versus Roadblocks (page 129) • Contributions I Hope to Make (page 131)	• Personal Mission Statement (page 133)

Week 6 completes Unit 3 on Tuesday and begins Unit 4 on Wednesday.

Outcomes and Evaluation See page 196. **Character Education Approaches: Asset-Building Focus, Aspirations Focus, Resiliency Focus** See page 197.

Unit 5 Gender Definition and Boundaries

Purpose

To identify the unique characteristics of boys and girls

To identify their own unique characteristics as growing men and women

To define appropriate and respectful boundaries between the sexes

To listen to the personal concerns of the opposite sex

Week 7 Activity Sequence

Monday	Tuesday	Wednesday	Thursday	Friday
Choose from the following activities: • Ideas About Men and Women (page 138) • Separate Tables (page 150)	• Media Images (page 139)	• Personal Banners (page 153)	• Situation Cards (page 144)	Reflections group, journal work, field trip, guest speaker, or videotape

Week 8 Activity Sequence

Monday	Tuesday	Wednesday	Thursday	Friday
• Personal Boundaries (page 152)	• How We'd Like to Be Treated (page 147)	• Fishbowl (page 146)	• What Does Respect Look Like? (page 149)	• Personal Attachments (page 109)

Outcomes and Evaluation See page 198.   **Character Education Approaches: Asset-Building Focus, Aspirations Focus, Resiliency Focus** See page 199.

Unit 6 Stewardship

Purpose

To evaluate the need for services within the school community

To create effective action plans to meet the unmet needs in the school community

To perform acts of service and stewardship

Week 9 Activity Sequence

Monday	Tuesday	Wednesday	Thursday	Friday
Choose from the following activities:	• Ideal School (page 160)	• Keep, Change, and Build (page 162)	• Action Planning (page 163)	• Peace Quilt (page 165)
• Card Castles (page 158)				
• Build Me a World (page 159)				

Outcomes and Evaluation See page 200.   **Character Education Approaches: Asset-Building Focus, Aspirations Focus, Resiliency Focus** See page 200.

Optional Culminating Activity

Create a rite of passage event by and for students and parents. This event should include a ceremony in which students give up a symbol of their childhood and accept a symbol of their entry into adulthood from their parents. This event should include a letter from all parents detailing their support of their children and their approval of their children's personal mission statements (see Rites of Passage and Initiation, pages 167-175).

Notes

Part One

Opening Quotation: Roger C. Mills, with Elsie B. Spittle, *The Health Realization Primer: Empowering Individuals and Communities* (Long Beach, CA: R. C. Mills and Associates, 1998), p. 3.

Chapter 1

Opening Quotation: Ralph Waldo Emerson, quoted in Adrienne Betz, *Scholastic Treasury of Quotations for Children* (New York: Scholastic, 1998), p. 63.

1. Charity James, *Young Lives at Stake: The Education of Adolescents* (New York: Agathon Press, 1974).

2. Jack Canfield and Mark Victor Hansen, *Chicken Soup for the Soul: 101 Stories to Open the Heart and Rekindle the Spirit* (Deerfield Beach, FL: Health Communications, 1993), p. v.

Chapter 2

Opening Quotation: Victor Borge, quoted in Dennis D. Embry, "The Science of Building Peace: How School Climate Can Prevent or Increase Substance Abuse and Violent Crime" (Tucson, AZ: Heartsprings, Inc. 1997; paper handed out at the National Training Associates' 1997 YES conference), pp. 5–6.

1. Thomas Edison, quoted in Adrienne Betz, *Scholastic Treasury of Quotations for Children* (New York: Scholastic, Inc, 1998), p. 63.

2. Roger C. Mills, with Elsie B. Spittle, *The Health Realization Primer: Empowering Individuals and Communities* (Long Beach, CA: R. C. Mills and Associates, 1998), p. 3.

Chapter 3

Opening Quotation: Marian Wright Edelman, quoted in Adrienne Betz, *Scholastic Treasury of Quotations for Children* (New York: Scholastic, 1998), p. 180.

1. Peter L. Benson, *The Troubled Journey: A Portrait of 6th–12th Grade Youth* (Minneapolis, MN: Search Institute, 1993) p. 7.

2. Russell J. Quaglia and Kristine M. Fox, *Believing in Achieving* (Orono, ME: National Center for Student Aspirations, 1998), p. 45.

3. Michael Grinder, *ENVoY: A Personal Guide to Classroom Management* (Battle Ground, WA: Michael Grinder & Associates, 1995), p. 2.

4. Raymond J. Golarz and Marion J. Golarz, *The Power of Participation: Improving Schools in a Democratic Society* (Champaign, IL: Research Press, 1995), p. 25.

Chapter 4

Opening Quotation: Muhammad Ali, quoted in Adrienne Betz, *Scholastic Treasury of Quotations for Children* (New York: Scholastic, 1998), p. 56.

1. Thomas Armstrong, *Multiple Intelligences in the Classroom* (Alexandria, VA: Association for Supervision and Curriculum Development, 1994), pp. 2–3.

2. Michael Grinder, *Righting the Educational Conveyor Belt* (Portland, OR: Metamorphous Press, 1991), pp. 19–21.

Chapter 5

Opening Quotation: Anne Frank, quoted in Adrienne Betz, *Scholastic Treasury of Quotations for Children* (New York: Scholastic, 1998), p. 107.

Part Two

Opening Quotation: Buddha, quoted in Stephen Mitchell, *The Enlightened Mind: An Anthology of Sacred Prose* (New York: HarperPerennial, 1993), p. 11.

Chapter 6

Opening Quotation: Jack Kornfield, *A Path with a Heart: A Guide Through the Perils and Promises of Spiritual Life* (New York: Bantam, 1993), p. 332.

Chapter 7

Opening Quotation: Rainer Maria Rilke, quoted in Stephen Mitchell, *The Enlightened Mind: An Anthology of Sacred Prose* (New York: HarperPerennial, 1993), p. 187.

Chapter 8

Opening Quotation: Russian proverb, quoted in Adrienne Betz, *Scholastic Treasury of Quotations for Children* (New York: Scholastic, 1998), p. 121.

Chapter 9

Opening Quotation: Ethiopian proverb, quoted in Adrienne Betz, *Scholastic Treasury of Quotations for Children* (New York: Scholastic, 1998), p. 53.

Chapter 10

Opening Quotation: African-American proverb, quoted in Adrienne Betz, *Scholastic Treasury of Quotations for Children* (New York: Scholastic, 1998), p. 62.

Part Three

Opening Quotation: Barbara de Angelis, quoted in Jack Canfield, Mark Victor Hansen, and Kimberly Kirberger, *Chicken Soup for the Teenage Soul: 101 Stories of Life, Love and Learning* (Deerfield Beach, FL: Health Communications, 1997), p. 211.

Chapter 11

Opening Quotation: Eleanor Roosevelt, quoted in Adrienne Betz, *Scholastic Treasury of Quotations for Children* (New York: Scholastic, 1998), p. 181.

Chapter 12

Opening Quotation: Marian Wright Edelman, quoted in Adrienne Betz, *Scholastic Treasury of Quotations for Children* (New York: Scholastic, 1998), p. 49.

Chapter 13

Opening Quotation: Michael Gurian, *The Wonder of Boys: What Parents, Mentors, and Educators Can Do to Shape Boys into Exceptional Men* (New York: Putnam, 1996), p. 131.

1. Ibid, pp. 151–53.

2. Carlton Coon, *The Hunting Peoples* (Boston: Atlantic, Little Brown, 1971), pp. 392–93. Quoted in Louis Carus Mahdi, Steven Foster, and Meredith Little, *Betwixt and Between: Patterns of Masculine and Feminine Initiation* (La Salle, IL: Open Court Publishing Company, 1987), p. xii.

Resources

Books

Angell, M. Cathy. *My Spirit Flies: Portraits and Prose of Women in Their Power*. Bellingham, WA: Bay City Press, 1997.

Armstrong, Thomas. *Awakening Genius in the Classroom*. Alexandria, VA: Association for Supervision and Curriculum Development, 1998.

Armstrong, Thomas. *Multiple Intelligences in the Classroom*. Alexandria, VA: Association for Supervision and Curriculum Development, 1994.

Benson, Peter L., Judy Galbraith, and Pamela Espeland. *What Kids Need to Succeed: Proven, Practical Ways to Raise Good Kids*. Minneapolis, MN: Free Spirit Publishing, 1998.

Benson, Peter L., and Carl D. Glickman. *All Kids Are Our Kids: What Communities Must Do to Raise Caring and Responsible Children and Adolescents*. San Francisco: Jossey-Bass, 1997.

Bodine, Richard J., Donna K. Crawford, and Fred Schrumpf. *Creating the Peaceable School: A Comprehensive Program for Teaching Conflict Resolution*. Champaign, IL: Research Press, 1994.

Brown, John L., and Cerylle Moffett. *The Hero's Journey: How Educators Can Transform Schools and Improve Learning*. Alexandria, VA: Association for Supervision and Curriculum Development, 1999.

Campbell, Joseph. *The Hero with a Thousand Faces*. Princeton, NJ: Princeton University Press, 1990 (reprint of 1949 edition).

Canfield, Jack, and Mark Victor Hansen. *Chicken Soup for the Soul: 101 Stories to Open the Heart and Rekindle the Spirit*. Deerfield Beach, FL: Health Communications, 1993.

Canfield, Jack, Mark Victor Hansen, and Kimberly Kirberger. *Chicken Soup for the Teenage Soul: 101 Stories of Life, Love and Learning*. Deerfield Beach, FL: Health Communications, 1997.

Collins, Chase. *Tell Me a Story: Creating Bedtime Tales Your Children Will Dream On*. New York: Houghton Mifflin, 1994.

Coon, Carlton. *The Hunting Peoples*. Boston: Atlantic, Little Brown, 1971.

Covey, Stephen R. *The 7 Habits of Highly Effective People: Powerful Lessons in Personal Change.* New York: Simon and Schuster, 1989; Fireside, 1990 reprint edition.

Crockett, Lib, and Jay Smink. *The Mentoring Guidebook: A Practical Manual for Designing and Managing a Mentoring Program.* Clemson, SC: National Dropout Prevention Center, 1991.

Emery, Merrelyn, and Ronald E. Purser. *The Search Conference: A Powerful Method for Planning Organizational Change and Community Action.* San Francisco: Jossey-Bass, 1996.

Goldberg, Mark F. *How to Design an Advisory System for a Secondary School.* Alexandria, VA: Association for Supervision and Curriculum Development, 1998.

Gregson, Bob. *The Incredible Indoor Games Book: One Hundred and Sixty Group Projects, Games, and Activities.* Belmont: Pitman Learning, 1982.

Grinder, Michael. *Righting the Educational Conveyor Belt.* Portland, OR: Metamorphous Press, 1991.

Gurian, Michael. *The Wonder of Boys: What Parents, Mentors, and Educators Can Do to Shape Boys into Exceptional Men.* New York: Putnam, 1996; Tarcher, 1997 paperback edition.

James, Charity. *Young Lives at Stake: The Education of Adolescents.* New York: Agathon Press, 1974.

Karns, Michelle. *DOisms: Ten Prosocial Principles That Ensure Caring Connections with Kids.* Sebastopol, CA: National Training Associates, 1995.

Karns, Michelle. *Ethnic Barriers and Biases: How to Become an Agent for Change.* Sebastopol, CA: National Training Associates, 1998.

Karns, Michelle. *How to Create Positive Relationships with Students: A Handbook of Group Activities and Teaching Strategies.* Champaign, IL: Research Press, 1994.

Kauth, Bill. *A Circle of Men: The Original Manual for Men's Support Groups.* New York: St. Martin's, 1992.

Kornfield, Jack. *A Path with a Heart: A Guide Through the Perils and Promises of Spiritual Life.* New York: Bantam, 1993.

Lewis, Barbara A. *What Do You Stand For?: A Kid's Guide to Building Character.* Minneapolis, MN: Free Spirit Publishing, 1998.

Lewis, Barbara, A., and Pamela Espeland. *The Kid's Guide to Service Projects: Over 500 Service Ideas for Young People Who Want to Make a Difference.* Minneapolis, MN: Free Spirit Publishing, 1995.

Lewis, Barbara A., Pamela Espeland, and Caryn Pernu. *The Kid's Guide to Social Action: How to Solve the Social Problems You Choose — and Turn Creative Thinking into Positive Action.* Minneapolis, MN: Free Spirit Publishing, 1998.

Mahdi, Louise C., Steven Foster, and Meredith Little, Eds. *Betwixt and Between: Patterns of Masculine and Feminine Initiation.* La Salle, IL: Open Court Publishing Company, 1987.

Mills, Roger C., with Elsie B. Spittle. *The Health Realization Primer: Empowering Individuals and Communities.* Long Beach, CA: R. C. Mills and Associates, 1998.

Mitchell, Stephen. *The Enlightened Mind: An Anthology of Sacred Prose.* New York: HarperPerennial, 1993.

Moore, Robert L., and Douglas Gillette. *King, Warrior, Magician, Lover: Rediscovering the Archetypes of the Mature Masculine.* San Francisco: HarperSanFrancisco, 1991.

Moore, Thomas. *Care of the Soul: A Guide for Cultivating Depth and Sacredness in Everyday Life.* New York: HarperCollins, 1992.

Pearson, Carol S. *Awakening the Heroes Within: Twelve Archetypes to Help Us Find Ourselves and Transform Our World.* San Francisco: HarperSanFrancisco, 1991.

Pipher, Mary. *Reviving Ophelia: Saving the Selves of Adolescent Girls.* New York: Ballantine Books, 1994.

Quaglia, Russell J., and Kristine M. Fox. *Believing in Achieving.* Orono, ME: National Center for Student Aspirations, 1998.

Quiroz, Hilda Clarice. *Start with the Kids: 5 Days to Building a Classroom Community.* Santa Cruz, CA: Education Training and Research Associates, 1997.

Roehlkepartain, Jolene L. *Building Assets Together: 135 Group Activities for Helping Youth Succeed.* Minneapolis, MN: Search Institute, 1995.

Weiner, Bernard. *Boy into Man: A Father's Guide to Initiation of Teenage Sons.* San Francisco: Transformation Press, 1992.

Weisbord, Marvin R., and Sandra Janoff. *Future Search: An Action Guide to Finding Common Ground in Organizations and Communities.* San Francisco: Berrett-Koehler, 1995.

Witmer, Judith T., and Carolyn S. Anderson. *How to Establish a High School Service Learning Program.* Alexandria, VA: Association for Supervision and Curriculum Development, 1994.

Organizations

Boys to Men Mentoring Network
9587 Tropico Drive
La Mesa, CA 91941
(619) 469-9599
boystomen@home.com EMAIL
www.mkpsd.org/btm/enter.html WEB SITE

Covey Leadership Center
Jamestown Square
Provo, Utah 84604
(800) 255-0777
www.covey.com WEB SITE

The ManKind Project
The New Warrior Training Adventure
The Woman Within
P.O. Box 230
Malone, New York 12953
(800) 870-4611
moreinfo@mkp.org EMAIL
www.mkp.org WEB SITE

National Training Associates
Reviving the Wonder Training
Reviving the Wonder Training of Trainers
P.O. Box 1270
Sebastopol, CA 95473
(800) 624-1120
info@nta-yes.com EMAIL
www.nta-yes.com WEB SITE

Index of Activities

Aces and Faces, 105

Action Planning, 163

Animal Heroes, 85

Asking Forgiveness, 116

Back to Back, 52

Body Part Connections, 104

Build Me a World, 159

Card Castles, 158

Characteristics I Admire, 127

Circles and Circles, 99

Circle of Life, 93

Circle of Support, 107

Clay Transformations, 67

Clearing a Conflict, 110

Contributions I Hope to Make, 131

Cross the Line, 65

Elder Circle, 148

Feelings Banners, 56

Fishbowl, 146

Frog Flipping, 101

Game of Life, 154

Gender Differences, 141

Generation Interviews, 88

Give Me a Lift, 108

Grab Bag, 55

Great Escape, 106

Hero Collage, 79

Hero Tales, 89

Heroes: Think, Feel, Act, 81

Heroic Mind Web, 80

Heroic Quotations, 77

Homemade Books, 40

How We'd Like to Be Treated, 147

I Got You Now!, 96

Ideal School, 160

Ideal School Chart, 161

Ideas About Men and Women, 138

Integrity, 69

Keep, Change, and Build, 162

Keeping Each Other Afloat, 62

Life Journey Map, 70

Local Heroes, 83

The Mask I Wear, 71

Media Images, 139

Mingle, Mingle, 100

Model Interview, 140

Outside/Inside Box, 73

Paper People, 49

Peace Quilt, 165

Personal Attachments, 109

Personal Banners, 153

Personal Boundaries, 152

Personal Brochure, 60

Personal Dreams, 124

Personal Mandala, 50

Personal Mission Statement, 133

Question Cards, 142

Reach Out and Touch Someone, 95

Reflection Group Discussion, 44

Reflections on Heroic Quotations, 78

Relaxation, Meditation, Contemplation, 42

Separate Tables, 150

Shapes, 94

Situation Cards, 144

Sticky Paper Heroes, 86

Strengths Versus Roadblocks, 129

Support Chart, 87

Sweet Talk, 48

Thank You Very Much, But I Gotta Go, 98

Timelines, 51

Tri-Fold, 63

What Do I Stand For?, 54

What Does Respect Look Like?, 149

What I Value in Life, 125

When Am I in My Power?, 58

You Send Me, 102

About the Authors

Ric Stuecker, MA, is a senior staff associate with National Training Associates. He has dedicated his career to challenging youth at risk to discover their inner strength and spirit and to make significant contributions to the community and world outside themselves. Since he was a young teacher, he has believed it is crucial that adults mentor youth and initiate them in meaningful ways into the adult community.

In addition to Reviving the Wonder retreats, Ric leads workshops in leadership, personal growth, study skills, and communication strategies for youth throughout the United States. He trains adults who teach and work with youth in resiliency and asset building, nonverbal communication and management, and presentation skills. He also trains trainers and coaches in these areas.

Ric inspired and initiated creative innovations in curriculum design and teaching for elementary and secondary students as curriculum coordinator and dean of faculty at the Saint Francis School just outside of Louisville, Kentucky. He instituted, developed, and directed the adolescent treatment center for chemically dependent youth at Our Lady of Bellefonte Hospital in Ashland, Kentucky. He is currently the primary consultant to the Youth at Promise initiative of the Archdiocese of Louisville, Kentucky, and a consultant to asset-building programs in the diocese of Toledo, Ohio, and in school districts in Idaho, Oklahoma, and California.

Ric lives with his wife, Barbara, in Louisville, Kentucky. He has two grown daughters living in Asheville, North Carolina.

Suze Rutherford has inspired youth throughout the United States with her powerful workshops and retreats. She dedicates her work with youth to the idea that all young people are geniuses and that it is our job as adults to inspire them and to empower them to greatness, no matter what we perceive as their difficulties or roadblocks.

Suze is a professional health education consultant who has worked in the field for more than two decades. She teaches stress management, nutrition, exercise, self-awareness, and communication skills to diverse lay and professional audiences all over the country. Recently, Suze has expanded her work to trainings designed to create safe environments free of bullying on school campuses. In addition, she leads retreats for adults, guiding them to revive their wonder, reconnect with youth, discover their inner spirit and revitalize their work.

Suze lives with her husband, Dan, in the Cascade mountains outside of Seattle, Washington. She is working on a children's book about her dog, Axel, and a book of real-life, inspirational short stories about and for youth.

About National Training Associates

National Training Associates (NTA), founded in 1982, is a training and consulting firm focused on fostering the social, emotional, and spiritual growth of youth. NTA consultants specialize in working with those dedicated to positive youth development, promoting resiliency, and asset building. Our consultants create learning experiences both directly for youth and for those who empower their growth at all levels of involvement from the individual school or youth program to state and national forums. We are dedicated to teaching and training the most effective skills and strategies for fostering healthy youth development and to establishing local capacity by promoting onsite expertise and resident coaches. We do this through workshops, seminars, youth summits, retreats, and skill laboratories. Our services include a full range of consulting practices from facilitating meetings to keynoting major conferences.

Reviving the Wonder Workshops, Retreats, and Training of Trainers

In the past five years, NTA has collaborated with local trainers, consultants, school personnel, and agencies in developing *Reviving the Wonder* experiences that address the specific needs identified by onsite experts. For school districts in a number of communities throughout the United States, NTA provides one- and two-day workshops for teachers demonstrating how to interweave the strategies in this manual into their daily teaching. In doing so, teachers are using the *Reviving the Wonder* activities to create optimal learning environments in their classrooms. We also create experiences for youth and adults. These include one-day, two-day, and three-day retreats for youth, renewal experiences for adults called *Reviving the Wonder in Adults,* and training of *Reviving the Wonder* trainers who can then provide these experiences in their local communities.

NTA can provide your school, agency, or community with a master *Reviving the Wonder* trainer who will design and implement a program for youth in your area. Our workshops for teachers train them to implement these strategies in their daily work with students. Additionally, we train individuals and teams to use the material in this manual and to create retreat experiences for youth that teach new skills and transform lives.

National Training Associates Contact Information

WEBSITE	www.nta-yes.com
PHONE	(800) 624-1120
FAX	(707) 874-0129
EMAIL	info@nta-yes.com
ADDRESS	P.O. Box 1270, Sebastopol, CA 95473